IMMANUEL

IMMANUEL

Outrageous Myth or God's Truth?

Perry Laukhuff

VANTAGE PRESS
New York

All biblical quotations are from the King James
Version, unless otherwise indicated.

FIRST EDITION

Published by Vantage Press, Inc.
516 West 34th Street, New York, New York 10001

Manufactured in the United States of America
ISBN: 0-533-09554-9

Library of Congress Catalog Card No.: 91-90844

0 9 8 7 6 5 4 3 2 1

To

my wife, Jessie, whose faith, encouragement, and discerning criticism made this book possible,

and to

the Rev. Fr. Anthony P. Treasure, latter-day apostle, whose eloquent teaching and contagious faith helped to destroy my agnosticism

Behold, a virgin shall conceive, and bear a son, and shall call his name Immanuel.

—Isaiah 7:14

Behold, a virgin shall be with child, and shall bring forth a son, and they shall call his name Emmanuel, which being interpreted is, God with us.

—Saint Matthew 1:23

Contents

Preface   xi
Introduction   xiii

1. Advance Notice   1
2. When Jesus Was Born   5
3. A Flight to Safety   9
4. Glimpse of Precocity   12
5. Prologue   18
6. Meeting Satan in the Wilderness   22
7. Choosing Messengers and Executors   28
8. The Exercise of Miraculous Power   33
9. Healing the Sick   39
10. Raising the Dead   47
11. Feeding the Hungry   51
12. Loving the Unlovable   56
13. Setting the Goals   61
14. Laying Hypocrisy Bare   66
15. "Whom Do Men Say That I Am?"   70
16. Foreglimpse of Heaven   73
17. A Farewell Dinner   77
18. Accepting the Inevitable   82
19. Tragedy: Betrayed, Reviled, Condemned   86
20. "Death"   93
21. "He Is Risen"—Immanuel's Triumph   98
22. Return to the Father   103
23. Postscripts from Heaven   106

Preface

The author is the first to wonder at his audacity in trying to write a biography of Jesus Christ, however modest. Surely the shelves of our libraries are already overcrowded with accounts of the life of the man whom Christians call "Lord and Saviour"? Surely another attempt from a theological nobody can have no useful purpose?

Nevertheless, I have felt strongly moved to make the seemingly uncalled-for attempt. In this little work, I have tried to focus rather strongly on the divine aspect of Christ's nature, while yet being as careful as possible to steer clear of anything that might seem to be an heretical separation of the two natures of Christ. I bear ever in mind and wholeheartedly accept the dictum of the Council of Chalcedon that our Lord was "truly God and truly man . . . recognized in two natures [but] not as parted into two persons. . . . " Depending on which of the two natures I am emphasizing at any given moment, I have generally referred to Christ as either "Jesus" or "Immanuel."

This slender essay is intended to awaken a meditative approach to the life of Jesus Christ. It is meant to be an easily understood account of his life, avoiding any narrowly theological approach. It is written by an Anglican layman to be read by any Christian and indeed by non-Christians. Only the reader can decide whether it fulfills its purpose and stimulates any fresh understanding of the man who gave new meaning to the teachings of the Law and the Prophets.

No one could be more astonished that the idea of undertaking this Immanuellian biography came into his head than the author himself (unless it be the author's wife!). As a boy, I was reared in the pious Arminian atmosphere of the no-longer-extant Church of the United Brethren in Christ, now merged with the United Methodist Church. In middle age, I became religiously indifferent, indeed rather thoroughly agnostic. My experience was in higher education and in the world of diplomacy. Theology was totally alien to me, and religious thought and worship played no part in my daily life.

Some few years after I had passed the half-century mark, unidentified and unidentifiable forces began to work in me and on me to pull me back into a definite relationship to God. The way was long, the process tortuous, not to say torturous! I had no Damascus Gate experience. I resisted strenuously. However, in the end, as I was approaching late middle age, I was drawn back ineluctably into the circle of believing and practicing Christians through Anglicanism.

Thus Immanuel came alive again for me after a long hiatus. I can only thank God, with some wonderment, that He has permitted me to write, in my later and more meditative years, this brief and no doubt somewhat partisan account of the life of His Son on earth. May others find it a useful stimulant for their faith or a useful lodestone if they are without a compass.

These remarks would be very incomplete were I not to acknowledge the editorial and scholarly debt I owe to two men whom I am proud to call friends. The Rev. Dr. Carroll E. Simcox in the United States and the Rev. Dr. E. W. Trueman Dicken in England gave generously of time, thought, and energy to read my manuscript and to encourage and correct me. These two eminent theological scholars have the cup of my gratitude filled high, pressed down, and running over.

Perry Laukhuff
Amherst, Virginia
Christmastide 1990

Introduction

This is the brief account of an outrageously unbelievable story—the life of God among men for a little more than three decades approximately two thousand years ago. A world-shaking event of this nature was foretold by the prophet Isaiah in the mid-eighth century B.C., and his prophecy was echoed eight hundred years later by the Evangelist Saint Matthew, one of the witnesses and companions of the Presence. Life has never been the same since.

The story is altogether incomprehensible except to the limited extent to which it can be described and interpreted by human minds and human languages. The Christian perceives it dimly as an extreme indication of God's love for mankind, a love so great that he "humbled himself to be born of a virgin," to share the joys and pain of human life and to die finally in a supreme manifestation of his love. By dying and then overcoming death he conferred on mankind the gifts of forgiveness and eternal life.

Not surprisingly, the non-Christian and the unbeliever find this story too much to accept. Some of its details are, of course, factual and historically demonstrable and cannot be disbelieved. Immanuel, the man called Jesus of Nazareth, *did* live and *was* put to death. But the interpretation of these two facts and the acceptance of many other details of the story depend largely on the faith of the believer. They also depend on the evidence and witness presented by the small band of Jesus' followers and especially by His closest disciples, the Apostles. That witness is of the most powerful. These disciples were mostly very ordinary, hardworking men. They observed Jesus; they heard Him talk; they traveled and ate with Him. For three rich years they saw Him as a teacher and a prophet. Until His death and Resurrection, they clearly had the utmost difficulty in understanding Him as Immanuel, "God with Us."

One of the most powerfully convincing arguments to me as a believer is the way in which these men changed after certain events that occurred at the end of Immanuel's sojourn on earth. Suddenly, they *knew*. Suddenly, they understood. Suddenly, they believed. Suddenly, they were transformed from the generally undistinguished and sometimes cowardly men they had been into men marked by extraordinary courage, extraordinary zeal, extraordinary effort and pertinacity, and extraordinary conviction.

These men, these witnesses, were totally convinced by events and their experience that they had known Immanuel. We know His life and His character and His love by their witness. Their conviction becomes our conviction.

This, then, is the brief story of their Immanuel, who is our Immanuel.

IMMANUEL

Advance Notice

In a figurative way, notice of God's coming human birth was given hundreds of years in advance when Isaiah, a man of vision close to Jehovah, looked into the future. Beginning his prophetic vocation in 740 B.C., he found it was his terrible task to warn the Hebraic people of the disasters soon to fall upon them. By way of comforting King Ahaz in particular and the Jewish nation in general, he gave an assurance—brief and almost casual—that a child would be born of a maiden and the child's name would be Immanuel, "God with us."

This was a prediction applicable to the fairly immediate future. Nevertheless, it had such overtones of the loving support and presence of the Lord that seven hundred years later Saint Matthew seized upon the same words and repeated them in the evident conviction that Isaiah's prophecy had been fulfilled with finality in the birth of Jesus Christ. There is more than a suggestion that in this interpretation he was mirroring things which Jesus Himself taught. (See, for example, Saint Luke 24:27.)

Thus, in one sense, Isaiah's prophecy was first fulfilled in the eighth century before Christ, but in another and greater sense it was fulfilled in the dawn of the Christian era. Centuries separated the two prophecies. Centuries also have passed since Saint James wrote that "the coming of the Lord draweth nigh." But our human conceptions of time are irrelevant and misleading when speaking of the working out of God's plans. Because God is eternal—because he is, was, and will be—all human ideas of time are inadequate in speaking of him and his plans for humanity. When we use such terms as *yesterday, today, tomorrow, ancient, modern, future, soon, nigh, in time, awhile,* and *forever,* we are limiting our perception and confusing our understanding of all that pertains to God.

Whatever Isaiah's meaning in the eighth century B.C., God was insistent upon a direct, special, and private announcement to the person most immediately concerned in the birth of our Immanuel. Gabriel, the messenger of God and angel of comfort to men, was sent to make this announcement. (You will remember that Gabriel is recorded in the Bible as having made at least two other visitations on earth, to Daniel and to Zacharias. One is left to wonder whether he might also have been the angel who wrestled with Jacob.)

The story is told in Saint Luke's Gospel. Gabriel addressed the maiden Mary very courteously and then gave the message to her with little preamble, straight from the shoulder, as it were. She would conceive and bear a son named *Jesus,* the "Son of the Highest," the "Son of God." In answer to Mary's perplexed confusion at such a revelation, the angel explained that this would be accomplished by the Holy Ghost. (This, by the way, is the second of seventeen references Saint Luke makes to the Holy Ghost.) It is not stated that Gabriel actually asked Mary whether she would accept his incalculable honor, but the implication is that he did, because she gave an answer and he waited to hear it.

Mary agreed. Her acquiescence has often been cited as a perfect and high example of human obedience to God. It is fascinating, though futile, to speculate on what would have happened had she refused! We may be sure that God would have found another way, another vessel for the conception and birth of His Son.

2

This scene of announcement, of advance notice, is so unparalleled that it has intrigued the minds of artists throughout Christian history. Painters have sought to depict it. (More recently, so have filmmakers, with much less satisfactory results.) Writers have strained the limits of vocabulary to do likewise. In truth, actual facts are scarce. Where was Mary at that moment? What was she doing? Just how did she react—with composure or with startlement—to this sudden visitation?

At the turn of this century, a brilliant but eccentric English writer, Frederick Rolfe (sometimes writing as Baron Corvo), told the story in a quaint and utterly charming and human way in his *Stories Toto Told Me*. The event is described through the imagination and words of a simple Italian servant boy, Toto, in a wholly fanciful but mundane way, as it would be conceived of by the peasant mind. Mary is pictured as sitting in her garden, surrounded by flowers, making her evening meditation. All was utterly silent and peaceful. When the announcement came, it was made in great human state. Suddenly, Mary was not alone; the archangels Gabriel, Michael, and Rafael knelt before her. Gabriel communicated his message as the others sang, "Ave," in low voices. When the trembling maiden gave her consent, a dove from heaven flew down and nestled in her bosom. The stars, "the army of angels," knelt before her. The accompanying archangels crowned her with a "lily diadem of pearls," and the angels kissed the violets at her feet. The embassage returned to paradise, and Mary lifted her hands, gave thanks to God, and made an offering of herself.

Fanciful in the extreme, yes. Touched with peasant mysticism and even superstition, yes. But it is an appealing attempt to put the unbelievable and the indescribable into colorful, artistic, and reasonably realistic human terms. Who knows? Perhaps it *was* that way!

At any rate, the biographical account starts here, in

Nazareth, in the sixth month of Mary's cousin Elisabeth's pregnancy with John the Baptizer. It was a private announcement, echoing the public announcement by Isaiah of an event to happen "soon." God wanted Mary to know and understand in advance, and he wanted her full acceptance and obedience. Immanuel's coming was imminent. God was, of course, already with us in spirit. He was only announcing his coming in human form for a human sojourn.

This cosmic event had no witnesses. It must be taken on faith or rejected because of the absence of faith. Saint Luke alone testifies to it, but he was not present and must have had it from Mary herself, whether at first, second, or third hand we do not know. She certainly believed and, rushing off to visit and confide in Elisabeth, gave expression to her belief in that glorious paean of praise, the Magnificat:

My soul doth magnify the Lord,
And my spirit hath rejoiced in God my Saviour.
For he hath regarded the low estate of his handmaiden:
    for behold, from henceforth all generations
    shall call me blessed.
For he that is mighty hath done to me great things;
    and holy is his name.

Full understanding, full acceptance, full praise and thanksgiving. Mary, the vehicle, was ready. The world did not yet know; Isaiah's prophecy was still just that, an indefinite prophecy. Only Elisabeth and Joseph are known to have heard the news—the former from Mary herself, Joseph from an angel.

4

2

When Jesus Was Born

The birth of the prophesied and announced Immanuel was secret; at least there is no record of witnesses. We don't know on what day of the year it occurred. We aren't even sure of the year, although the evidence (references to Augustus, Herod, and Cyrenius) suggests that it was before the year 4 B.C. We don't know at what hour of the day or night it occurred, although again the evidence (the story of the shepherds) suggests that it was at night. We assume Joseph was present; was there also perhaps a midwife? There was no public health office, no bureau of vital statistics, to record the birth officially.

All we have is a simple, beautiful story told by Saint Luke, who was certainly not there, and it would seem he must have gotten such details as he gave from Jesus' mother herself. Saint Matthew merely states that "when Jesus was born" wise men came from the east to Jerusalem. Saint John limits himself to the theological statement that "the Word was made flesh and dwelt among us."

Saint Luke, therefore, tells us essentially all that we know about this event, which was to change the life of the world. It is hard to think of a single happening of any great importance at all that was not better recorded and chronicled. Saint Luke does inform us that the birth took place in Bethlehem, located in the obscure little Palestinian tetrarchy or kingdom of Judea,

5

under Roman rule. It took place there because Joseph had to go there for the first census ordered by the Emperor Augustus. Joseph had actually been living in Nazareth, in the northern district of Galilee, but all had to return for the census to the hometown of their family.

We are told that he took his pregnant wife, Mary, with him, and this is of significance as showing that Joseph accepted her as his wife even though she was not pregnant by him. It gave legal status both to her and to the child to come. The town was crowded; the inn's regular accommodations were full. The exact quarters in which the birth took place are not named, but Mary "laid [the babe] in a manger," thus suggesting that He was born in some dependent building or sheltered portion of the inn's courtyard in which animals were wont to be quartered.

And that is the sum total of what we know of the arrival of God among us in human flesh.

It is not much. It would be very easy to reject it as unauthenticated, as a story, a myth, a tale circulated among early Christians, a mere invention to be used as a prop for the extravagant claims of the new religion. But we do know that there was an historical figure named Jesus. The account of the birth is straightforward and with no claim by Saint Luke of anything miraculous or supernatural about the birth itself. It was an ordinary human birth, and there is no substantial reason to doubt or reject it. Actually, the only parts of the biography of Immanuel that depend for acceptance in some measure on faith as opposed to fact are the Annunciation, the miracles, the Transfiguration, the Resurrection, and the Ascension. We will deal with these matters of faith as we go along.

There are two outside events connected with the birth. First, there were the shepherds, simple men watching their sheep in the fields outside Bethlehem. Saint Luke tells us that an angel announced the birth to them as that of a Saviour.

6

Accompanying this announcement, they heard the song of angels proclaiming glory to God and peace to all men "who enjoy his favor" (as the Jerusalem Bible translates it). The shepherds came to the manger and saw the babe and then went out and told others what they had heard and seen.

Saint Matthew records the other, less immediate, connected event. "Wise men," men "from the east," men who studied the stars and read messages into them, saw a star which somehow carried the message to them that a "King of the Jews" had been born somewhere to the west. They traveled to Jerusalem, made inquiries of King Herod the Great (thereby arousing great concern and fear in the King's mind), and went on to Bethlehem. There they found the child in a house, no longer in a manger, presented the gifts they had brought, and "fell down and worshipped him."

We may well wonder at all these circumstances. Here is a cosmic event if ever there was one—the advent of God into this human and mundane and material world. Mary and Joseph separately learned from angels of its imminence. Elisabeth heard of it from Mary. Shepherds heard of it from an angel. Some townsfolk or countryfolk in the area heard some version or other from the shepherds. The Magi deduced it from a star, and Herod heard of it from the wise men. Saints Matthew and John reported the bare fact of the birth. Saint Luke reported it briefly, with only a few details, in a homely and almost poetic way.

How strange this all is. Accustomed as we in the twentieth century are to sensations, blaring announcements of everything from assassinations to royal weddings to natural catastrophes to fire sales, it is hard to understand why God would proclaim the arrival of his Son, co-equal and co-eternal in substance, in such a limited and modest way. It would seem that in some form or other there should have been universal trumpets, earthquakes, signs and portents, visions and voices, for the whole earth to see and hear.

But no, that was not and is not God's way. He does not need the trappings of authority, much less the tinsel of public relations, to assert himself and emphasize his doings. He is God and Father-Creator, who existed before the world or time were, who made and loves man, who is grieved by man's disobedience and folly, but who will not coerce man, who gives man free will and the right to accept or reject God.

Of his great love for us, he came among us that day or night in Bethlehem—long ago in our terms, *now* in his terms. He gave the signal and the record to those ready and willing to believe. The rest he left to the developing record of his Son's life, words, actions, and return to him. Immanuel's subsequent life is the important part of the story. It had to begin somewhere, so it began in Bethlehem with the birth of a very human little baby already proclaimed to be the Son of God, Immanuel, "God with us."

This birth marked man's second chance.

3

A Flight to Safety

Herod the Great was crafty, cunning, and cruel. He sent the wise men off to Bethlehem to find the prophesied King of the Jews and report back to him. He wanted a name, an identity. No report came back and Herod was furious. Not having a name, he struck at a group. His soldiers killed all male children up to the age of two in Bethlehem and the area roundabout. This was the famous Slaughter of the Innocents, and justly infamous as well. It is a curious irony and paradox that Herod's cruelty still impresses the mind of man twenty centuries later in the midst of an infinitely greater slaughter of innocents slightly younger.

Herod was crafty. So crafty, in fact, that he should have realized he could not thwart the coming of the promised Immanuel. And, of course, he didn't. Joseph had a dream that he interpreted as a message from God conveyed by an angel. And who shall say it was not? The people of Biblical times may have been unsophisticated by our lights, but they were very open to God and any communication from him. Today our minds are closed to God and open only to scientists who wire patients up with electrodes and study them and their dreams as they sleep! Who today would think for a minute of going to Egypt because of an uneasy dream!

Joseph, however, had no hesitation. The angel of his dreams (Gabriel again?) told him that the infant Jesus was in danger from Herod and that safety lay in flight to Egypt, where they should stay until told to return. So strong was the sense of divine warning that Joseph immediately got up, awakened Mary, and fled with his family secretly in the dark hours of the night. In Egypt they stayed, but exactly how long and how they lived there we are not told by Saint Matthew, whose Gospel is our only account of this exile. Perhaps Joseph plied his carpenter's trade to make a living. Perhaps, as Jewish tradition has it, the Holy family lived at Heliopolis, near modern Cairo. We do not know.

All we know is that in the inexorable working out of God's plan his Son was saved from the slaughter. In due time, Joseph had another dream, another visit from the angel-messenger. Herod was dead, and the way was now clear to return. But Joseph heard that Herod's son and successor, Archelaus, reigned in Judea. This made him so fearful even yet for the child's safety that he returned to Nazareth in Galilee, instead of to Bethlehem in Judea.

Jesus, being a mere baby, can have remembered nothing of this travel/exile episode. It had no discernible influence on Him—save of course to spare Him for His adulthood and His mission to man. It is nevertheless instructive to reflect upon the two roles of Egypt in Judeo-Christian history. The first Joseph, sold into slavery there, proved, in the working out of God's plan, to be the instrument of Israel's salvation from famine, when Jacob and all his sons and their families fled to Egypt. In due course, Israel was led back out of Egypt through the guidance of Moses. Then, some twelve hundred years later, Israel was again led to safety in Egypt by another Joseph; one can say "Israel" because Jesus was the very embodiment, in God's plan, of Israel. This exile was short, and the child's "father," Joseph, simply continued in his role as father and led Jesus, the new Israel, back to the homeland. There is thus a dual parallelism between two incidents far separated in time but very similar in significance. God watched over Israel (the family of the patriarch Jacob) in the time of Joseph/Moses, and again he watched over Israel (his Son, Jesus) in the time of Joseph and Mary and the Incarnation.

A mere biograhical footnote in the temporal life story of Jesus, though rich with significance in the eternal story of God, this brief interlude made all the rest of the Christian narrative possible. It really tells us nothing at all about Immanuel. It tells us a great deal about God, and it also tells us a great deal about the unquestioning way in which Joseph was always ready to obey God without hesitation. With regard to Herod's part in it, it tells us that however free we are to ignore God, we are not free to intervene in the working out of his plans. To those who doubt God's immanence, his presence in the life of this world, this story should give pause for thought.

4

Glimpse of Precocity

It has always been a strange thing to me that Jesus' early life story is so void of detail, almost blank. Here is Immanuel, God among men, and until His ministry begins when He is about thirty years old we have only six brief glimpses into His life, if most of them can be called even that! We are told about His birth, we hear about the visit of the Magi, we learn that He was circumcised after eight days and presented in the Temple when He was forty days old, we know that His family fled to Egypt for His safety, and then we have the account of His encounter with the learned doctors in the Temple.

Nowadays we are accustomed to having the childhood lives of the great and the famous recounted exhaustively in their biographies. Thus, at first glance, it seems curious that we have such exceedingly meager scraps of information about the early life of God Himself on earth.

What were the relationships in the family? How was He educated? What was He like as a boy? Did He have a lot of childhood friends, and did He participate normally in the play and games of the neighborhood children? Was He serious, lighthearted, introspective, or an extrovert? What signs were there of His unique nature? Did He help His carpenter father? What did He do for a living and by way of preparation all through His twenties? What, if anything, did He know of the angelic revelations to His mother and father, of Elisabeth's spontaneous Ave Maria, of His mother's exultant Magnificat of thanks and praise, or of Simeon's grateful Nunc Dimittis? These and other questions crowd into our minds—at least, have always crowded into my mind—and I have longed for the illumination of more knowledge.

However, we have to be content without the answers. The four Gospels, after all, are not and do not pretend to be biographies. They are, rather, records of His acts and teachings. They are expositions of His purpose. They are instructional, not biographical. And so we must be content with only one brief glimpse of the child, the boy. In its very limited way, it is a most revealing glimpse.

His parents, being good, traditional, and devout Jews, went to Jerusalem every year for the Feast of the Passover. In this particular year, when the boy Jesus was twelve years old, they made the usual Passover pilgrimage. This occasion must have evoked poignant memories in Mary and Joseph of their own earlier flight for refuge to Egypt, the exact reversal of the exodus of the Jews from Egypt which the Feast bore in sacred remembrance. Saint Luke's account (Chapter 2) does not say how long they stayed in the capital ("when they had fulfilled the days" were his words), but normally it was a seven-day Feast. At any rate, Mary and Joseph eventually began their return journey north to Nazareth.

Everyone else started to return home at the same time, so that their road to Galilee, like all roads out of Jerusalem at that moment, was clogged with long lines of returning pilgrims. In the crowd and confusion, Mary and Joseph did not at first note the fact that the boy—who must have been well-grown and quite capable and self-sufficient by that time—was not actually with them. When His absence was noticed after perhaps a few minutes or even several hours, the parents at first assumed that He was with relatives or friends somewhere in the long, straggly train of people. Unworried, they seem not really to

13

have looked for Him during the first day's travel. Then they began looking, but "they found him not," and so in great anxiety they turned back to Jerusalem.

One can imagine the worried search, probably increasingly frantic, up and down the streets of the city among places they had visited or where they had stayed, the anxious inquiries made of acquaintances, even of strangers, shopkeepers and so on. At long last, after three days, it seems they thought of looking in the Temple precincts, and there, indeed, the lost One was found. And what was He doing, this twelve-year-old? Was He perhaps seeing the sights with friends His own age? No, He was engaged in learned discourse with "the doctors," the intellectual leaders, the teachers, those who were expert in theology, philosophy, and the history of Israel. The scene is one which really boggles our imagination. It is as if a twelve-year-old boy from Ipswich, Massachusetts, had come to Cambridge and barged in on an open forum of philosophical discussion by a dozen of the most rarefied minds of Harvard University!

Jesus is reported to have been both listening intently and putting sharp questions to the group. Probably a large group of visitors to the Temple were standing around listening, at once entranced and perplexed by a discussion rather beyond their understanding at times, wondering at the audacity of this young boy and yet compelled to admire the extraordinary keenness of a mind so young which could yet engage on equal terms with the cream of Jewish intellect and insight in the very citadel of Jewish learning and worship, the Temple. The Biblical account emphasizes the astonishment felt by the onlookers at the depth of knowledge and dexterity of expression displayed by the youngster.

One is devoured by curiosity to know what subjects were being discussed. Were they talking about the history and significance of the Passover? Was Jesus inquiring about the promises God had made to Moses and the people of Israel? Was He perhaps discoursing on the prophecies of a Messiah to appear and to lead the Jewish people? Was He defending the rule of Spirit against the rule of Law? We shall never know.

His parents, taut with anxiety and yet weak with relief at finding Him, did what any parents would have done under the circumstances. They upbraided Him; they remonstrated with Him; they demanded some explanation for His failing to join them on the journey. Quite understandably, they poured forth the feelings of worry He had caused them over the last three or four days. His only reply on record was the question: "Wist ye not that I must be about my Father's business?" This was scarcely understandable or helpful to them, and in cold print it even looks unfeeling and harsh, not to say disrespectful.

Mary had been forewarned. Joseph had been forewarned. Yet when this extraordinary boy talked about His "Father's" business, they were taken aback and at a loss to know what He was talking about. Twelve years of being with Him, twelve years of knowing that He was in some extraordinary way "God with us," had still not been enough to enable them to cope with this reply.

They returned to Nazareth, and with their return the curtain falls for eighteen more years over the life of Immanuel.

As we ponder this tantalizing mise en scène, we are struck by several impressions. One is that at so young an age Jesus apparently had acquired some understanding of His special nature, His special relationship to God. He had quite evidently not just been helping his father, running errands for his mother, and playing tag with the boys of His neighborhood. He had quite evidently been doing much deep thinking, turning over in His mind whatever His mother may have told Him about His birth, studying the Scriptures, considering the prophecies of old, trying to come to terms with the problem of His future role. Without a background of such interior research, He simply could not have taken on "the doctors" in what amounted to a public seminar. This boy had had and always would have a quite remarkable, if not unique, inner life.

Was He actually impudent, harsh, and unfeeling toward His parents, as a surface reading of the incident seems to show? Not at all. Only the *theologically* significant reply is quoted in Scripture. He undoubtedly would have set an example of love and compassion in this as in all things. He undoubtedly added words of contrition and begged His parents to understand what inner forces had caused Him to behave in this seemingly neglectful way. Saint Luke confirms this in a short but meaningful phrase: "And he went down with them, and came to Nazareth, and was subject unto them." He did not go home with the family in surly rebellion. He did not run away. He did not turn into a problem child. He went along as bidden "and was subject unto them."

How revealing is this single glimpse into the life of Jesus before His short ministry! What we see here is precocity, early recognition of His nature, intelligence far beyond His years, the ability to attract, astonish, and influence people—but with it all the kind of loving submission to parents which we would expect God to exemplify and teach, were he among us.

There is something else we cannot fail to notice about this story. The account begins and ends with words that convey almost the same message about Jesus, confirming all that we instinctively draw from the scene. Prefacing the story, Saint Luke tells us that "Jesus grew, and waxed strong in spirit, filled with wisdom: and the grace of God was upon him" (Saint Luke 2:40). Surely it can be no mere coincidence that at the conclusion of the story we are told that "Jesus increased in wisdom and stature, and in favor with God and man" (Saint Luke 2:52).

In those two phrases is really all we need to know about the first thirty years of Jesus' life, illuminated as they are only by the one brief glimpse of His encounter with the doctors in the Temple. He was moving within His destiny and His mission with sure steps. Under the all-watchful eye of the Father, God's Son was growing like a normal human being; He was being observed affectionately and admiringly by His fellowmen. At the same time, He was also developing His singular relationship to God the Father, an extraordinary capacity for understanding, and an extraordinary ability to communicate His message.

Through grace, God was with Him as well as in Him.

5
Prologue

God had a cousin—on the human side, of course—a second cousin, it would appear. Mary's cousin Elisabeth, who was beyond the years of childbearing and had never had children, miraculously bore a son, John. The birth of this child was foretold to his father, Zacharias, by an angel of the Lord, Gabriel, standing beside the altar in the Temple.

The parallelism here is obvious and simply shows that God has plans and is very thorough and consistent in carrying them out. The coming of Immanuel and the coming of His precursor, John, were both announced to the Hebrews by the prophet Isaiah, hundreds of years in advance. Then the conception of both and their imminent advent were announced by angels, to the mother in one case and the father in the other.

As the two boys were cousins, it would seem that they would have known one another as children, yet the Scriptures give no indication of this. Also, it would seem that each would have heard something about the supernaturally predestined vocation of the other, yet again there is no specific record that either was aware of the task assigned to the other.

John seems to have lived in the wilderness very simply, almost like a hermit, for at least a part of his youth and young manhood. Then suddenly some inner signal was given and he began to exercise a kind of prophetic ministry in the Jordan valley. He preached a doctrine of repentance and also charity, for he told people to give to the needy, to act fairly and honestly, and to be peaceable and just. He especially exercised a ministry of baptism as a symbol of the washing away of the sins of which people repented.

Multitudes of people of all sorts and degrees flocked down to Jordan to hear him preach. Disciples gathered around him. He was regarded as a prophet; many even speculated that he might be the Christ, the Messiah, the Saviour and Lord of Israel, who Isaiah had predicted would come. But John always made it crystal clear that he was not that Messiah but merely his forerunner and servant, "the latchet of whose shoes I am not worthy to stoop down and unloose," as Saint Mark puts it in 1:7. (How that striking phrase of humility has burned itself into our minds!) Again and again John explained that he only came to prepare the way for one greater than he. He explained again and again that his baptism with water was important but that the prophesied one would baptize with the Holy Ghost. As Saint John was to put it, in another memorable and pregnant phrase, John the Baptizer came "to bear witness of the Light"; "he was not that Light, but was sent to bear witness of that Light" (Saint John 1:7,8).

John never departed by one iota from the task God had laid upon him. Crowds swarmed about him. He was respected, revered, and viewed with almost holy adulation. How easy it would have been for him to claim that he was indeed the man of prophecy, the Messiah. Instead, day after day, with complete fidelity, he proclaimed the might of the One who would come after him.

Finally, one day, that One appeared before him and sought baptism. John was reluctant, saying that it was rather he himself who should receive the greater baptism that Jesus could give. In the end he gave in to Jesus and baptized Him. Then came that sign from heaven—the dove descending, the

19

voice proclaiming that this was the Son, "in whom I am well pleased" (Saint Mark 1:11).

Did John really know Jesus as both his cousin and as the Chosen of God? And at what point? There is no clear evidence. The testimony is, in fact, somewhat confusing. One would suppose that each man would have known about the other from their mothers if from no one else. Each had been heralded by angelic announcements. John's mother, Elisabeth, certainly knew about the nature of Mary's son, for she greeted Mary as "the mother of my Lord" (Saint Luke 1:43). On the other hand, it was widely and publicly known that Zacharias, John's father, had prophesied that his child would be "the Prophet of the Most High" and would prepare the way for the Lord. So there is every inherent reason to suppose that each child knew something of the special nature of the other.

The fact that John was reluctant to baptize Jesus confirms this. Certainly after Immanuel's baptism by John the latter knew Jesus' identity, because Saint John's Gospel records that John the Baptizer declared he knew Jesus as "the Son of God" because he saw the dove descend upon Him at His baptism (Saint John 1:32–34). Indeed, even as he saw Jesus coming toward him, he exclaimed, "Behold, the Lamb of God, which taketh away the sin of the world" (Saint John 1:29). It is really unimportant to know at what precise moment the two recognized each other's identity. Clearly there was an innate recognition, a spark of current flowing between the two that bound them spiritually together from the beginning as lesser and greater, as precursor and Saviour of the world.

John was clearly the more open of the two to all the doubts that assail the strongest human faith. When he sat in jail as Herod's prisoner, he had doubts. Suddenly he was not sure. *Was* this Immanuel? He heard wonderful stories of healings and miracles. But how could he be sure? So he sent two of his own disciples to ask Jesus straight out, "Art thou he that should come? Or look we for another?" And they returned with fresh testimony to John of healings. God is infinitely patient and reassuring in the face of our doubts and lack of faith.

There is another somewhat strange incident recounted of the way in which John pointed out Jesus to two of his disciples as "the Lamb of God," whereupon they left him and followed Jesus. One was Andrew, who went to fetch his brother, Peter, the pair of them being promptly summoned to follow Jesus as disciples and Apostles. In all this there is some confusion of accounts between the Gospels of Saints Matthew, Mark, and Luke on the one hand and Saint John on the other. But in this connection, time relationships or just who said what at what point are unimportant.

The important thing in all this is that God sought, through John, to prepare his people—or those of them that would believe—for the coming ministry of Immanuel. Not all people are capable of understanding. God knows that. Not all people are prepared to reach out to God in response to his reaching out to them. God knows that. But for those who earnestly seek him, for those who will weigh and accept the evidence, God reveals himself. He wanted to give those willing souls every chance to know, to hear, to understand, and to be prepared.

Thus it was that before Immanuel came and until Immanuel had become a grown man and was at last prepared to exercise His ministry, God spoke a Prologue through his chosen vessel, John. John's influence and reputation were enormous. His name and his message were on everyone's tongue. Pharisees, publicans, the ordinary man in the street— all knew of this Baptizer. A sense of expectation grew strong, as God intended.

The way was now prepared.

Meeting Satan in the Wilderness

The time for ministry and revelation had come. Saint Luke (3:23) tells us that Jesus had reached the age of thirty. He whose baptism would be unto salvation had submitted Himself to the baptism of John, the baptism of repentance and cleansing (forgiveness). Then there had to occur a strange interlude of reflection, self-examination, and self-testing. He had to come to terms with His extraordinary mission before He could set about it.

Coming up from the Jordan after His baptism and the benison of God's voice and dove, He retired into the "wilderness," probably the desolate and wild hill country above the Jordan valley. "Then," says Saint Matthew (4:1), He was led into the wilderness. "Immediately," says Saint Mark (1:12), He was driven into the wilderness. Whether led or driven, it is clear from both accounts, as well as that in Saint Luke's Gospel (4:1–13), that He was moved to this period of retreat by the Spirit, by God within Him, and that this was an essential preliminary in God's design.

We know that Jesus fasted. *Fasting* is an inexact term, meaning variously either complete abstinence or partial abstinence from food. We are not told exactly to what extent our Lord fasted during His forty days in the wild. It is possible that He abstained altogether, but this would have been an exercise so severe and debilitating that I have always

22

preferred to think that He ate just enough to sustain life. (It must be noted, however, that Saint Luke asserts specifically in Chapter 4, Verse 2, that the Lord "did eat nothing"; on the other hand, both Saint Matthew and Saint Mark say angels "ministered unto him," which could include provision of some food.)

It is curious that I have always thought of this retreat as a period of prayer and meditation. Actually, the Scriptural story does not mention prayer. Nevertheless, prayer was so usually associated with fasting that we may assume it in this case. Certainly, introspective meditation was a purpose of this time apart. Jesus was making a final effort to understand Himself and His role.

How did He live? It may have been in a cave or perhaps a brush structure or even just under the open sky. It must have been hot and uncomfortable in the daytime and cold and uncomfortable at night. There was even a certain element of danger, for it was an area where "wild beasts" roamed, as Saint Mark notes. The authors of the first three Gospels must have received the story of this whole episode from Jesus Himself. Thus it must have come firsthand that He fasted, that there were wild beasts, and that angels took care of Him. Also that there He met Satan.

For Satan is a central character in this history. He is referred to variously as the devil, as the Tempter, and as Satan. But there he was, this fallen angel, the prince of devils, this evil antagonist of God whom Jesus was later to call "the prince of this world." The devil had recognized already his great adversary, and he sought an early opportunity to win Him over or discredit Him. And so, for forty days and forty nights, he sought a chink in the armor of God.

One may wonder how it is possible to tempt God, to trip him up. The trouble revealed by this kind of speculation arises from the great difficulty we have in dealing with the dual nature of this Jesus. If He were solely God, of course, it is impossible to conceive that He would be subject to ordinary human temptations or could remotely be open to attack by Satan, one of his own creatures. If He were solely man, it is equally inconceivable that He could emerge totally unscathed, that He could resist *all* temptations. It is almost impossible for us to grasp in any real way the idea that God and man can be united inseparably in one Person. But because they were, He was tempted in entirely human ways *and* with the strength of God was able to contemptuously repel the temptations.

We do not know all that He was subjected to in the way of evil enticement while He came to final grips with His nature in the wilderness. The story tells of three great temptations, perhaps only as samples or examples. He was hungry, and a hungry man dreams of all sorts of delectable dishes. He was aware of His extraordinary powers—and so was Satan. Thus it came into His mind to turn stones into "bread." This mirage was dealt with by recalling that one truly "lives" by the word of God, not by bread. Satan had no answer.

Next, as Jesus pondered His extraordinary inner power, Satan had an easy opportunity to put it into His mind that He could be Satan's deputy and rule all the kingdoms and nations of the world if only He would agree to give Himself over to devil-worship. Jesus was quick to remember and quote the Scriptural Mosaic commandment to worship the Lord God only. Satan had no answer.

Knowing that Jesus was debating in Himself how best to carry His message to the world, Satan next suggested a publicity stunt to end all publicity stunts. The Lord should simply throw Himself off the highest spot of the Temple, relying on angels to catch Him, and thus at one stroke establish at the center of Hebrew worship and beyond the peradventure of a doubt that He was indeed God with us. Again the devil was rebuffed, with Moses' injunction not to tempt God. Again Satan had no answer.

The Tempter departed, defeated in this first and greatest of his encounters with Christ. There is evidence, however, that Satan never completely gave up, but hovered always nearby, ready to seize any opportunity to overthrow God. We note in Saint Luke 22:53 that in the hour of His arrest in the Garden Jesus felt the presence of "the power of darkness."

We see, then, that during His days in the wilderness Jesus met and vanquished the temptations of the flesh (self-gratification through bread), worldliness (rule of the world under Satan), and pride (self-glorification through pulling off a great trick to impress people). Meeting and rejecting these temptations, He confirmed His own understanding of Himself as the Son of God, enjoying God's full support even in moments of greatest human weakness. What an essay in bravery, in testing oneself to the utmost at a moment of supreme physical weakness! He was to do it again on the Cross.

Several things impress themselves upon me in reading this story of the encounter of good and bad, of God and Satan, of God's strength and man's weakness. These words are being written in an era when doubt and change and compromise are in the air and Christ's followers are being subjected to latter-day temptations. Attempts have been made to revise the Lord's Prayer with regard to the phrase "and lead us not into temptation." I am no student of Greek or Latin, of Hebrew or Aramaic, and so I do not know what words the original texts ascribe to our Lord in this part of His prayer. The objection has been raised that God would never lead his children into temptation. Well, it cannot help but strike one at once in reading the story of Christ's meeting with Satan in the wilderness that God did in fact lead his own Son into temptation. "Then was Jesus led up of the spirit into the wilderness to be tempted of the devil," records Saint Matthew (4:1)—and Saint

Luke records it in the same language. Even the modern versions, such as the Jerusalem Bible and the New English Bible, which bend a little to the currents of modernism in the Lord's Prayer and give us "do not put us to the test," have to admit that "Jesus was led by the Spirit out into the wilderness to be tempted by the Devil."

Surely there is nothing strange or unfatherlike about this. The world is full of evil, full of temptation. A father who spares his child all unpleasantness, all trial, is going to rear a spoiled weakling, whose eventual fall will be fearful. God is well aware of that danger. Temptation is going to come our way, and our response to it, our yielding or resistance, is going to shape our character and determine our worth. Even Immanuel had to face temptation and prove, by repelling Satan totally and decisively, that He was the Son of God and worthy to redeem the world. It is surely evident that this single incident at the beginning of His ministry proves conclusively the indissoluble union of the human and the deific in Jesus the Christ.

One is struck in this story, too, by the first of many evidences (leaving aside the implications of the encounter with the doctors in the Temple) of Jesus' deep familiarity with the Scriptures as they then existed in the Old Testament. To every one of Satan's temptations Jesus responded with quotations taken from the sixth and eighth chapters of Deuteronomy. How discomfited Satan must have felt, for he too, sly Old One that he is, had himself displayed his knowledge of the Scriptures by buttressing one of his temptations (the third one) with a line from Psalm 91!

We are led, too, to ponder the example of fasting which Jesus set for us in this extraordinary episode. Fasting as a spiritual and religious discipline has fallen into desuetude in these latter days. People fast only in order to reduce their weight or use fasting for its publicity value as an instrument of protest to make a political point! The fact is that religious and spiritual leaders, mystics and teachers in all ages, from Moses to Gandhi, have known the value of a fast. The sparing use or deprivation of food, at least up to a point, seems to sharpen the awareness, set free the mind and spirit, and enable one to get a clearer hold on the eternal verities. Jesus' forty-day fast may have weakened Him physically, but it weakened Him not a whit morally or spiritually and indeed sharpened His memory of the Scriptures and strengthened His grip on their meaning. One does not need physical strength to resist the Tempter; one needs mental clarity and moral strength. As one separates the heart and soul and mind from the physical body, one achieves a new strength of spirit.

So it was in this case. Immanuel proved Himself and His strength. He submitted Himself to a variety of very common human temptations. He fasted for strength. He vanquished the enemy. At the end, He "returned in the power of the Spirit into Galilee." His ministry began with Himself. He was now ready to emerge into the glare of public ministry.

7
Choosing Messengers and Executors

It is of little use to try to determine exactly what Immanuel did at the very outset of His ministry. The chronology of the Gospel record is too uncertain and to some extent conflicting. It does appear that after the wilderness experience He went to Galilee and specifically to Nazareth, His home town. No doubt He had determined a course of action while in the wilderness.

First He began to teach and preach, bringing His message directly to the people. He taught in the synagogues at Nazareth and at Capernaum on the Sea of Galilee. Probably, indeed almost certainly, He moved about to other places, too, to begin meeting the people and spreading His gospel of repentance, forgiveness, love, faith, and eternal life. He also began to heal on occasion and to perform other miracles.

Thus His fame began to spread abroad and He could start to think of gathering together some disciples, some particularly close followers. One man, especially such a One, could do much and range far and wide, but obviously disciples who were enthusiastic converts could magnify His eventual outreach many times over. Whether from observation and meetings or from sheer chance (although it is doubtful that God leaves his plans to sheer chance), Jesus commenced the process of choosing and gathering the inner circle about Him.

One day He was walking along the shore of the Sea of

Galilee, or the Lake of Gennesaret or the Sea of Tiberias, as it was variously called. He saw fishermen's boats and got aboard one belonging to a man called Simon, later known as Peter, "the rock." They pulled off, and after preaching to the crowd on shore, Jesus told Simon to let down his net. Simon was tired; he had been fishing all night without much success. Nevertheless, there was something about this man's voice, His eyes, His manner—or just possibly Simon recognized Him and knew of His preaching and miracles—something that bade obedience. Simon let down the net and took in so many fish that he had to call for help from fellow fishermen nearby. When the fish were brought to the shore, Jesus told Simon and his brother Andrew, who was with him, to follow Him and fish for men. They did, without recorded question, argument, or hesitation.

One account indicates that James and John were among those who helped Simon and that they were also summoned to follow Jesus and did so. Other accounts indicate that He encountered these two a little farther along the lake shore. In any event, they too abandoned their work and their livelihood without hesitation.

It may be noted that of the twelve who became Apostles, there is an account of the calling only of six: these four—Simon, Andrew, James (later known as James the Great), and John—and Matthew and Philip. Matthew was a publican, a collector of taxes or tolls, a class of men generally hated because they collected (or extorted) all they could, keeping a hefty commission for themselves. Matthew's name was actually Levi. Jesus was simply passing by, saw Levi, and with His ability to assess instantly the worth of a man told Levi to follow Him. Like the others, Levi (henceforth known as Matthew) "forsook all" and followed as bidden.

The finding and calling of Philip are recorded in equally

laconic terms, and Philip's response was equally immediate and decisive. What compelling power Immanuel had!

This is really the sum total of all we know about the choosing of the inner circle, the men later to be known as Apostles, those sent, messengers of the Lord. The other six, along with the six named above, are listed in the tenth chapter of Saint Matthew's Gospel, the third chapter of Saint Mark's Gospel, the sixth chapter of Saint Luke's Gospel, and the first chapter of the Book of the Acts of the Apostles. We know their names and, for the most part, not much else; they appear but seldom in the Scriptural accounts. They were Bartholomew, James (called "the Less," son of Alpheus), Thomas (also called Didymus), Simon (also called the Canaanite or Zelotes, to distinguish him from Simon Peter), and Judas, also called Jude or Lebbaeus or Thaddeus, to distinguish him from the twelfth, who was Judas Iscariot.

This was indeed a motley and seemingly undistinguished group of men. Four, at least, were commercial fishermen. One was a tax gatherer. The others are unidentified as to calling. A few are mentioned a number of times in the Scriptures—Simon Peter, John ("the disciple whom Jesus loved"), and of course Judas Iscariot, who betrayed Jesus and must be suffering eternal spiritual torment because of his action. Most of the others are mentioned only once or twice, and at least one, Bartholomew, is never mentioned outside the listing of Apostles.

These men seem to have lived with Jesus, tramped the countryside with Him, listened to His sermons and talks, and been the recipients of much private talk and revelation. Yet they were very slow to understand Him. They must often have been a disappointment to Him; sometimes He must have been tempted to despair of them. Peter swore vehemently at the high priest's house after Jesus was arrested that he did not know Jesus. Philip had understood so little that he asked the Lord to

30

show them the Father, which brought a sorrowful reproof from the Father's Son. None of them believed the first reports of the Lord's Resurrection. Thomas wouldn't even believe the reports of the other ten but stubbornly demanded to see for himself; pitying him, Jesus said, "Be not faithless, but believing." James and John were so far from understanding the spiritual nature of the Lord's kingdom that they besought His promise that they should sit on His right and left sides when He came into His glory; His rebuke moved the other ten to vociferous indignation against the two place seekers. They all went to sleep in the Garden as He prayed and waited for His fate. And, of course, there was the searing iron of the moment of His betrayal by Judas. Yes, He must have been tempted to despair of these men at times.

As disciples during His lifetime, these twelve seem to have been patently ineffective pupils and helpers. As far as we know, they were faithful, except for Judas and Peter's denials and the apparent absence of all of them except John at the Crucifixion. The trouble was that they just could not understand the new spiritual and moral thrust of the old Messianic prediction. Jesus must have been grieved and disappointed at times, but He never gave up on them. He explained and taught and pleaded and chided. He knew that He had chosen well. (The choice of Judas Iscariot may seem to be something of an enigma, though even he was undoubtedly part of God's plan and his example certainly shows most strikingly how even "the elect" may use their freedom of will to go to the bad.) Jesus was content to let the Gospel message marinate, so to speak, in their minds and spirits. He knew that they (except for Judas) would ripen in understanding and service. He was content to leave them behind as His administrators, His executors, the shepherds of His flock. He knew they would not fail Him.

And fail Him they did not. Slow to understand, of no seeming special abilities, they were transformed eventually by

31

the suffering and death of their Master, by His Resurrection and reappearance to them, and by the way in which He left them and "ascended" into some heavenly realm. Perhaps most of all they were inspired and reinvigorated, they gained understanding, courage, and zeal from the fulfillment of His steadily repeated promise that He would send One to lead and guide and sustain them. They became giants in the faith, fearless and tireless protagonists in the story of Immanuel, willing martyrs when it came to that. Never has a greater, more striking, or more successful transformation occurred. To me, this transformation has always been one of the key proofs of the truth of the Gospel.

Immanuel had to provide for the long future, knowing that He would be with us in physical person for only a brief lifetime. The success or failure of His plan rested on the shoulders of twelve frail men. He knew these men. Except for one, who was duly replaced, they lived up to every expectation. Immanuel's plan succeeded; His vision was superlatively correct; His faith was justified. Against the ultimate day of His return, He built His Church on the supporting pillars of these men.

8

The Exercise of Miraculous Power

From the beginning to the end of His earthly ministry, Immanuel is reported to have "performed" (as we say) miracles. That is, He did acts that do not seem to permit of normal explanation, which lie outside normal experience, acts that do not seem to fit into the laws of nature as we know them. These acts can be described in various ways: awe-inspiring, confusing, purposeful, seemingly without rhyme or reason, symbolic, compassionate. In other words, it is clear that the recorded miracles—and how many others are not described to us?—paradoxically raise doubts and skepticism in our minds because they clash with our normal human experience and knowledge of natural laws while they strengthen our belief that Jesus was in truth God with us.

We cannot tell the life-story of Immanuel without recording these miraculous acts and coming to grips as best we can with their truth and their meaning.

C.S. Lewis has defined a miracle as "an interference with Nature by supernatural power." He admits this is not the definition many theologians would give, but he defends it with his usual power, clarity, and conviction. Far be it from me to take issue with C.S. Lewis. However, in my own mind, I prefer to think of a miracle as an event which *seems* to be an interference with nature or natural law by an outside force but in reality, is simply an application of that natural law which is as yet outside our knowledge. This should really not be beyond our ability to accept. For centuries—and never more than in this twentieth century—man has been widening his knowledge of nature and its workings. Would not a tenth-century man have considered an electric light a miracle? Would he not have so considered a computer, a laser beam, an artificial heart, and hundreds and hundreds of other inventions and discoveries that subsequent research has brought within the circle of our understanding of nature and its workings? Is it therefore so impossible to think when Jesus walked on water or caused a dumb man to speak or brought Lazarus back to life He was simply applying principles still not discovered by us? If I am wrong about this, it is still quite possible to accept the miracles on the basis that C.S. Lewis suggests, that is, as new creations of God or an interference by God with laws and matter that he himself created and is master of.

At any rate, the scriptural record shows a large number of acts by Jesus which seem to fall in the category of miracles, actions beyond our ordinary experience and understanding and seeming to demonstrate powers not possessed by us. These miracles were of three main types: (1) the healing of illness of some sort, (2) the restoration to life of those who had died, and (3) extraordinary acts of all other descriptions. For discussion at the moment let us consider the third group, consisting of twelve (possibly only eleven) incidents.

It is probably not without significance that the first miracle took place at the very outset of Jesus' ministry, very likely soon after His emergence from the temptation experience in the desert. He was at the town of Cana in Galilee and was a guest at a wedding. The wine ran out and when His mother called this fact to His attention He made the cryptic reply, "Mine hour is not yet come." He was apparently not quite sure that He should yet make Himself and His power and nature known to the public. After a moment's reflection, Jesus evidently concluded that the occasion and the opportunity were made to order. At His direction, the servants filled six twenty- to twenty-five-gallon water pots with water. When some of this liquid was taken to the host, it proved to be wine of a superior quality. It is not recorded that anything was said publicly about this amazing event, but the disciples somehow learned of it and "the disciples believed on him."

He seems to have used His power for several different purposes. In a number of cases, like that of the wine at Cana, the purpose may be inferred to be to demonstrate to His disciples that He was truly the Messiah they were expecting. This same purpose was served by the two occasions on which He directed disciples to absolutely tremendous catches of fish. The first time, it was with Peter and Andrew and the effect was so powerful that they decided on the spot to follow this man as pupils and adherents. The same thing happened after His Resurrection, when He wanted to convince the Apostles that He was, beyond peradventure, the Risen Lord. This latter happening is told with such precision that we even know there were exactly 153 fish caught (Saint John 21:11)!

A similar purpose seems to have been served by Jesus' calming of the storm on the sea late one evening, because afterward the disciples asked each other "what manner of man is this?" (Saint Luke 8:25). And again, when He walked on the stormy waters toward the disciples struggling with the oars and bailing desperately, He was using His remarkable knowledge of the laws of physics (or, if you and C.S. Lewis prefer, His supernatural power!) to carry conviction to men who had seemingly forgotten about or been unimpressed by the feeding of five thousand men earlier that same day (Saint Mark 6:52). He made His point, at least for the moment; they "worshipped him saying, of a truth thou art the Son of God" (Saint Matthew 14:33).

On other occasions, He seems to have been using

miracles to convince the wider public. His claim to be the Messiah was so hard to believe that something striking was needed to reinforce it. And so, when confronted with five thousand hungry people who had patiently listened to His lengthy preaching, He found enough food for all of them (and twelve basketfuls over) in five loaves of bread and two fish. Incidentally, the subsequent feeding of the four thousand may be simply an altered and duplicating account of this same event.

Still another purpose of certain miracles may have been simply self-preservation, arising from His knowledge that His work was not yet completed, His "time" not yet come. This sort of miracle is exemplified by the incident which followed His teaching in the synagogue at Nazareth, when He had indicated that He was the anointed one of whom prophecies had been written. His hearers were incredulous and so angry at such claims from the mere son of Joseph the carpenter that they led Him out to a high cliff to throw Him over it. "But he, passing through the midst of them, went his way" (Saint Luke 4:30).

An incident quite similar to the foregoing took place once in the Temple, when the Jews were so infuriated at what they regarded as Jesus' blasphemous answers to their questions—almost their cross-examination—that they prepared to stone Him to death on the spot. "But Jesus hid himself, and went out of the Temple, going through the midst of them, and so passed by" (Saint John 8:59). Now in cases like these, if your faith is weak and you are determined to play the skeptic, you can contrive explanations other than the miraculous. You can say that Jesus had extraordinary powers of character or psychology, that He faced down the crowds, mesmerized them, overawed them to the point of forcing them to draw back and let Him pass through safely. Yes, you can say this, but even this evasion of the miraculous really accords Him such miraculous power that the evasion becomes pointless. On any reading, something quite beyond the normal took place.

It is not without significance, and this is a point to which I shall return again, that on the occasions of three of these assorted miracles (the cursing of the fig tree, the calming of the storm, and the walking on water) Jesus brought in the question of faith, chiding the disciples for their lack of it. In the latter two cases He used words like "where is your faith?" (Saint Luke 8:25) and in the instance of the fig tree He told them that they too could work miracles, "if ye have faith, and doubt not" (Saint Matthew 21:21). In passing, we may admit (I, at least, admit) that the cursing of the fig tree simply because it had no fruit on it out of season is almost beyond explanation. Possibly it was a symbolic act predicting the barrenness, the unfruitfulness, the disasters and near withering away of the Jewish people (in the 1930s and 1940s?). But this story, in the form in which it has come down to us, has defied any certain explanation by even the best theological minds. Perhaps it was simply a peg on which to hang the promise of similar power for others if enough faith existed.

It would seem, then, that these divers miracles were meant chiefly to aid Jesus' ministry by demonstrating power so unusual that people would be forced to believe in Him as the promised Messiah, the Son of God. Sometimes they did or seemed to for a while: "and there went out a fame of him through all the region round about" (Saint Luke 4:14). Again, the results of miracles were fleeting in the extreme. When the soldiers, guided by Judas, came to arrest Him in the Garden, Jesus had only to face them and to say, "I am he," to cause them to move back and fall to the ground, momentarily powerless, but they recovered on the instant and on His second admission of his identity they shackled Him and led Him away.

With the disciples, the miracles seem to have served their purpose somewhat better. They at last acknowledged Him to

37

be the Son of God; they "worshipped" Him. Even though their understanding of what they meant by their words and actions was far from complete until after the final miracles of the Resurrection and the Ascension, sealed by the descent of the Holy Ghost, it was a sufficient start.

After all, Immanuel was Himself a miracle. And I well know that faith, the acceptance of the unseen, the unknown, the "impossible," is the hardest thing in the world to acquire and to keep.

Notes

The miracles of assorted nature referred to in this chapter are:

1. Tribute coin in fish's mouth—Saint Matthew 17:24–27
2. Escape from Nazarenes—Saint Luke 4:28–30
3. First draught of fish—Saint Luke 5:1–11
4. Water into wine at Cana—Saint John 2:1–11
5. Escape from stoning in the Temple—Saint John 8:59
6. Repulse of soldiers in the Garden—Saint John 18:5–6
7. Second draught of fish—Saint John 21:4–12
8. Fig tree cursed—Saint Matthew 21:19; Saint Mark 11:13
9. Calming of the storm—Saint Matthew 8:23; Saint Mark 4:37; Saint Luke 8:22
10. Walking on water—Saint Matthew 14:25; St. Mark 6:48; Saint John 6:19
11. Feeding the five thousand—Saint Matthew 14:15; Saint Mark 6:30; Saint Luke 9:10; Saint John 6:1
12. Feeding the four thousand—Saint Matthew 15:32; Saint Mark 8:1

9
Healing the Sick

One of the most frequent miracles worked by Immanuel was that of healing the sick. No fewer than twenty-three specific acts of such healing are reported in the Gospels. In addition, it is apparent that He healed scores or more likely hundreds, even thousands, of other cases not individually mentioned. Saint Matthew makes a statement typical of similar ones by Saints Mark and Luke: "And Jesus went about all Galilee . . . healing all manner of sickness and all manner of disease among the people. And his fame went throughout all Syria: and they brought unto him all sick people that were taken with divers diseases and torments, and those which were possessed with devils, and those which were lunatick, and those that had the palsy; and he healed them" (Saint Matthew 4:23–24).

It is quite obvious that Jesus did not simply possess some kind of fancy snake oil or herbal remedy. He possessed some power which came of knowledge so advanced that we haven't begun to approach it for all our marvelous strides in serums, medicines, surgery, organ transplants, and the use of prostheses. His knowledge was evidently deep and profound, for He treated all sorts of bodily afflictions: fevers (perhaps bacterial or viral infections), blindness, dumbness, deafness, paralysis, withered limbs, crippling disability (perhaps including osteoporosis), deformity, leprosy, fluid accumulation (dropsy), and mental illness, to name most of those afflictions specifically identified in the New Testament. This was no flash in the pan, no fluke of quick recovery. This man, this Jesus, possessed *knowledge* of the human body. He possessed power unknown in His time or in ours. If you prefer, He possessed supernatural power, power held and conferred by God the Father-Creator.

It is fascinating to look at a few samples. Two blind men followed Him, hearing that He passed by, and besought His mercy. He asked if they believed that He could help them. They said yes; He touched their eyes and they saw again (Saint Matthew 9:27–31). There are at least four other cases of restoring sight recorded by Saints Matthew, Mark, Luke, and John. Restoration of the organs of sense and communication seems to have been especially frequent. Thus a deaf man with an "impediment of speech" was brought to Jesus. He put His fingers in the man's ears, touched the tongue with His own spittle, looked up to heaven, said, "Ephphatha" ("be opened"), and the man heard and spoke (Saint Mark 7:31–37). Something obviously happened on that occasion that is quite beyond the reach of our present-day medical science.

In Cana, Jesus met a nobleman from Capernaum who asked His help on behalf of his son, lying at death's door at home from a fever. Jesus made a cryptic pronouncement. "Except ye see signs and wonders, ye will not believe." The father begged His intervention once more, and Jesus told him his son "liveth," that is, was healed. The father went his way and was met by servants reporting the boy's recovery at the very hour Jesus had spoken (Saint John 4:46–54). It should be noted here that this is one of several healings carried out at a distance from the sufferer, without personal contact. The power that was involved was either supernatural or extremely advanced.

There is explicit reference to power in another case. A woman had been hemorrhaging for twelve years. Desperate, and having heard of the works of this man, she managed to get close enough in the crowd to touch the hem of His robe as He passed by. She was instantly cured. Jesus was "aware that power had gone out from him" (Jerusalem Bible) and asked who had touched Him. The woman was frightened but admitted it was she who had made the contact (Saint Mark 5:25–34).

Once, when Jesus was preaching in a synagogue somewhere in Galilee, there was in the congregation a man whose hand was withered and useless. Jesus saw him, told him to come forward and stretch out the hand, and pronounced it whole (Saint Luke 6:6–10). Withered limbs, paralyzed limbs, bent bones—He cured them all, with a skill and power denied to modern orthopedists, chiropractors, and osteopaths, to say nothing of surgeons.

Leprosy, the dread scourge of that and many other ages, succumbed equally to His power. A leper came to Him in Galilee, knelt before Him, and begged for his merciful help. The Lord touched him and commanded him to be clean. He was instantly cleansed of this loathsome disease (Saint Mark 1:40–45).

Fascinating is the account of Jesus' encounter with the madman of the tombs. Saints Mark and Luke say there was one man, Saint Matthew says two, but no matter. This man went about naked, slept in the tombs, and could not be restrained, for when put in chains and fetters he always broke loose, being very strong and violent. Jesus saw that he was possessed by devils, demons, or unclean spirits such as some people in our times call poltergeists. Jesus commanded the demons to leave the man. For some reason known only to the demons, they asked that they be permitted to enter into a herd of swine nearby, to which the Lord assented. They entered the swine, which promptly went mad and rushed down a steep cliff into the lake and were drowned. This story brought into

41

our language the picturesque "Gadarene swine." But the event was far more than picturesque. The lunatic was healed, his sanity returned, and people from all over that area swarmed out to see Jesus and the notorious madman now clothed and sane (Saint Matthew 8:28–34; Saint Mark 5:1–16; Saint Luke 8:26–40).

The list could go on, but these samples are enough to prove that Jesus was Immanuel, God among men. If you accept God's promise to send his Son, if you accept the account of the announcement by Gabriel to Mary, if you accept the account of the nativity at Bethlehem heralded by a star and an angel chorus, then you know from the healings that this was Immanuel. If you reject all the premises, you toss the healings aside as fictitious. But they were witnessed by the Twelve, they were witnessed by the converted disciples, they were witnessed by the hundreds and thousands who followed Jesus about, listened to His teaching, and saw the miracles. Many, many of these thousands were still alive when the Gospel accounts were set down in writing, thus making permanent and concrete what had at first been oral tradition. The Gospels would have been laughed to scorn as fairy tales had they been fabricated, but there is no record of any contemporary denials of their accuracy. It is therefore rational to accept the miracles as fact and as evidence that they were the work of Immanuel.

One may ask why Jesus healed and whether any common themes run through the accounts of the healings. First and foremost, the healings must be seen as a fruit of God's immeasurable love for man; they must also be seen as Jesus' exemplification of His Second Commandment: "Love thy neighbor as thyself." He loved, pitied, and sought to help everyone He saw who suffered physically, mentally, or emotionally. One cannot doubt this, for the miraculous healings fit so admirably and completely into the Lord's whole web of teaching, His entire message of love, of wholeness, of war on sin.

In fact, the Gospels confirm this view quite specifically. In at least four instances dealing with specific cases and in other passages where the account is more general, the record says that the reason for the healing was "compassion." When Jesus healed the leper, He is reported as being "moved with compassion" (Saint Mark 1:41). When the two blind men called out to Him from the roadside for help, "Jesus had compassion on them" (Saint Matthew 20:34). There were other cases, but one need not press the point. There was divine love at work here.

The same love was at work in the rebuke Jesus gave to violence when the ear of the high priest's servant was cut off by one of His enraged followers on the occasion of Christ's arrest in the Garden of Gethsemane. "And he touched his ear and healed him" (Saint Luke 22:51).

There is another striking element revealed in many of the cases of healing. Christ clearly attributed the healing—or at the very least His readiness to heal—to the *faith* of the one healed. Again and again He referred to this attribute. When the woman with the hemorrhage touched His garment, He turned to her and said, "Thy faith hath made thee whole" (Saint Matthew 9:22). When the Syrophoenician woman (the woman of Canaan) fell at His feet and begged Him to heal her mentally ill daughter and He found by interrogation that she had true spiritual understanding, He told her, "O woman, great is thy faith: be it unto thee even as thou wilt" (Saint Matthew 15:28). When the disciples complained to Him that *they* could not seem to do these miraculous healings (Saint Matthew 17:20) and asked why that was, He minced no words but said it was because of their unbelief: "If ye have faith . . . nothing shall be impossible to you." It seems quite clear, then, that faith, belief, played a key role in the healings.

43

Man must meet God with faith; in response, God meets man with love, healing, and forgiveness. The men who let the paralytic down through the roof, that he might get near enough to implore Jesus' help, had a faith that Jesus recognized and to which He responded by healing. To the healed He said, "Son, thy sins be forgiven thee" (Saint Mark 2:5).

It is evident, then, that in this process of healing there were not only advanced knowledge and extraordinary power at work, but there was also a mixture of attitudes and attributes involved—compassion, love, faith, penitence, and forgiveness. When the Apostles later understood this complex mix of ingredients, they too were able to heal (Acts 3, 5, 8, 9, etc.).

Sometimes Jesus seems to have used the power of healing to drive home a point about faith, about sin, about the excesses of Jewish legalism and worship of "the Law." On more than one occasion He appears deliberately to have healed on the Sabbath. Each time He did so, the Pharisees attacked Him for breaking the laws about the Sabbath. Each time He took occasion to drive home to His critics the absurdity of their position. He was particularly fond of pointing out that any of them would rescue his ox or his ass that might fall into a pit on the Sabbath, so why should not one much more help a human being in distress? Generally, there is no record of the effect of His retort on His adversaries. Occasionally, however, He did shame the critics in this way, as happened when He cured the woman who for eighteen years had been so bent over that she could not straighten up: "And when He had said these things, all his adversaries were ashamed" (Saint Luke 13:17).

We can speculate endlessly about Christ's motives; I certainly cannot fully read them. Sometimes He seemed to want to teach. Sometimes He seemed to want to convert. Sometimes He seemed to want to show people who He was. Sometimes He seemed to want to attract crowds so that He could reach more people. Sometimes part of His motive was quite obscure. Why, for instance, did He in at least three specific recorded cases tell the person healed to go on his way and say nothing about it to any man? (In any event, they never obeyed this injunction!) After all the speculation and after all the questions, the primary motivation insistently presses itself upon my own mind: He acted from compassion, from love for His people.

Certainly He never performed a miracle of any kind as a stunt. He never did these things for mean or unworthy reasons. He never acted to help evil, but only to help those with faith, those who threw themselves on His mercy, those whose spiritual eyes could be opened by His action. He never used miracles for punishment. He used His power only as one would expect a true Immanuel to use his power—as an instrument of unfathomable love. In the process, He proved yet again that He *was* Immanuel.

Notes

The citations for twenty-three specific reported healings are as follows:

1. Two blind men—Saint Matthew 9:27–31
2. Dumb man—Saint Matthew 9:32–33
3. Deaf and dumb man—Saint Mark 7:31–37
4. Blind man—Saint Mark 8:22–26
5. Woman with bent back—Saint Luke 13:11–17
6. Man with dropsy—Saint Luke 14:1–6
7. Ten lepers—Saint Luke 17:11–19
8. Malchus's ear restored—Saint Luke 22:50–51
9. Nobleman's son with fever—Saint John 4:46–54
10. Cripple at the pool—Saint John 5:1–9
11. Blind man—Saint John 9:1–7
12. Syrophoenician woman's devil-possessed daughter—Saint Matthew 15:22–28; Saint Mark 7:25–30

13. Centurion's servant with palsy—Saint Matthew 8:5–13; Saint Luke 7:1–10
14. Blind and dumb man—Saint Matthew 12:22; Saint Luke 11:14
15. Demoniac man—Saint Mark 1:23–27; Saint Luke 4:33–37
16. Peter's mother-in-law with fever—Saint Matthew 8:14–15; Saint Mark 1:30–31; Saint Luke 4:38–39
17. Gadarene demoniac—Saint Matthew 8:28–34; Saint Mark 5:1–17; Saint Luke 8:26–37
18. Leper—Saint Matthew 8:2–4; Saint Mark 1:40–45; Saint Luke 5:12–15
19. Woman with hemorrhage—Saint Matthew 9:20–22; Saint Mark 5:25–34; Saint Luke 8:43–48
20. Paralytic—Saint Matthew 9:2; Saint Mark 2:3–5; Saint Luke 5:18–20
21. Man with withered hand—Saint Matthew 12:10–13; Saint Mark 3:1–5; Saint Luke 6:6–10
22. Man's demoniac son—Saint Matthew 17:14–18; Saint Mark 9:14–27; Saint Luke 9:37–42
23. Blind men—Saint Matthew 20:30–34; Saint Mark 10:46–52; Saint Luke 18:35–43

10

Raising the Dead

What is death? Modern medical science has discovered many wonderful things, but the fundamentals still elude it. There is much dispute over the exact conditions which signify that a person is dead. Is it when the heart ceases to beat? Formerly it was thought so, but now life is sometimes revived after there is no discernible heartbeat. Is it death when the brain ceases to function and gives out no electrical impulses? Yet sometimes the brain seems dead, but the heart beats.

We read constantly of cases in which a "dead" person is revived. Not too long ago there was a report of a young boy who was immersed in the icy waters of a river for fifteen minutes. His temperature was far below that of a "living" person. He had no pulse. He did not breathe. There were no signs whatever of life. Yet he lived. Are such cases not miracles? Once we would have said so, yet today they are simply ascribed to the advances of medical science and skill.

Why then should it be difficult to accept the miraculous revivifications accomplished in Palestine two thousand years ago by Jesus Christ? He healed the impossibly sick and crippled. Why not accept His ability to call back to life? It may be alleged that in the recorded instances in which He raised people from the dead there was simply a mistake and the person was not actually dead. However, in the instance of Lazarus, it should be remembered that the man was four days dead, had been bound hand and foot with the grave-wrappings and entombed, and that his family rightly feared that decomposition had already set in. There is no room to suppose that he was not in all truth dead. In any case, our medical men today revive persons in whom all life signs are absent. So, obviously, did Jesus. We have here, then, further evidence that He had all knowledge, hundreds and thousands of years in advance of His times, knowledge and power that could only have come from God, the fountainhead of all life and knowledge.

There are three recorded occasions on which Jesus brought back to life persons who had died. In the three cases, the circumstances were rather strikingly different.

The first occasion was apparently rather early on in His ministry. He had gone to a town in southern Galilee called Nain in the course of His itinerant preaching and teaching. By sheer chance, it would seem, a dead man was carried out through the city gate at the very same moment as Jesus was entering the city through the gate. The mother—the man was an only son—was there, weeping. Jesus saw all this and was touched with pity. He reassured the mother, went to the bier, and told the dead young man to get up and so restored him, living, to his mother. All who witnessed this scene were awestruck, praised God, and looked upon Jesus as a "great prophet."

At apparently about the same time (though this is uncertain), Jesus was in the vicinity of Nazareth, still in Galilee. A "ruler" or synagogue official, Jairus by name, begged His help for his daughter, who was lying at death's door. Jairus obviously had great faith in this man Jesus, worker of wonders. Jesus went to the official's house, where the daughter had meanwhile died. He told the mourners that the girl was not dead "but sleepeth" and was laughed at for His pains.

However, He went in to the twelve-year-old girl and took her by the hand and she arose and walked.

The third case is astonishing in all respects and by any test. Jesus received word that Lazarus, the brother of His two devoted disciples at Bethany, Mary and Martha, was desperately ill. The sisters besought Jesus' immediate assistance. Very curiously, He delayed going for several days. Then came word by Martha that Lazarus had died and she reproached Jesus for not coming while her brother yet lived. So did Mary, who subsequently went out of town to meet Jesus as He approached. Jesus was deeply troubled by this news and possibly by these reproaches and hastened to the place of entombment. Ordering the stone that blocked the tomb to be removed, the Lord prayed in strange words that indicated He wanted those standing near to hear His conversation with the Father in order to cause them to believe in Him.

There followed the famous scene when He summoned Lazarus in a loud voice to come forth. (Notice that in this case He addressed Lazarus by name. Had He not done so, all the dead in that place would have arisen at His command! In the other two instances, He was in the presence of only one deceased person.) Lazarus did come forth, although the imagination is at a loss to picture the scene, as he was still bound from head to foot with "grave-clothes." At Jesus' word, he was unbound and so rejoined the living. Many conversions followed—and also much plotting by the unconverted chief priests and Pharisees.

These were the three miracles of raising to life of the dead. There is no discernible pattern to them. In one case, Jesus went immediately in response to a request, healing the woman with an issue of blood en route and stressing in both miracles the role played by faith. In another case, He seems to have acted on the spur of the moment out of sheer pity and sympathy. In the third case, He inexplicably delayed taking action when otherwise He might have prevented death, was clearly deeply moved with personal grief, yet is reported to have acted more in order to induce belief in Him than from any other motive.

Did Jesus raise still others from the dead? Quite possibly, although there is no indication of other life-restoring miracles, as there is in the various statements that He went about healing people in large numbers, in addition to the particular healing cases recorded. We shall never know precisely why He acted in these three specific instances, nor whether or why these were the only ones. A mixture of reasons was doubtless at work—compassion for and love of His people, a demonstration of the power and reward of faith, and a driving determination that people should understand who and what He was.

He was love personified, the love of God for man, whether dear friends or strangers were involved. He was power and knowledge personified, power and knowledge far beyond the ken of man. He was Immanuel, God at work among us.

Notes

The following are the citations for the three recorded cases of raising from the dead:

1. Son of the widow of Nain—Saint Luke 7:11–17
2. Jairus's daughter—Saint Matthew 9:18–19, 23–26; Saint Mark 5:22–24, 35–43; Saint Luke 8:41–42, 49–56
3. Lazarus—Saint John 11:1–46

11

Feeding the Hungry

Jesus was keenly aware that food, eating, is an absolutely essential requirement for the sustaining of life, any kind of life. Thus it comes about that food and eating were prominent items in His life and teaching.

He appears to have had no settled home of His own after He began his ministry.[1] He seems to have stayed with Mary and Martha and Lazarus frequently when He was in the vicinity of Jerusalem. There, in several recorded instances, and undoubtedly in many unrecorded ones, He had His meals, often in the company of His disciples and others. But it was not His own home, and so in a sense He did no conventional entertaining as host. He did not provide the food.

There seems actually to have been only one occasion (possibly two) on which Jesus literally provided food for the hungry. That was when He took a few scraps and multiplied them miraculously into enough food to feed five thousand hungry people who had been listening to His preaching all day. (The second possible occasion would have been when He fed the four thousand, if one does not accept the common assumption that this was simply a different version of the feeding of the five thousand.[2])

There was, of course, the all-important meal in the Upper Room on the night before His Crucifixion. Here Jesus gave bread and wine (there may well have been other food) to His disciples. However, this time the purpose was not primarily to feed the physical body. Rather, the feeding was symbolic; He was concerned with sustaining the spiritual strength of His followers then and through the long future. This duality of thought concerning food and drink was to run throughout the examples and teachings of Christ. As man, He was keenly aware of the necessity of food and drink to sustain life. As God, He was just as keenly aware that the spirit, too, needs constant sustenance if its flame is to be kept burning.

There were several marginal instances in which Jesus was concerned with providing food or drink. In the first of His miracles, He turned water into wine to the very human end that the guests at the wedding in Cana should slake their thirst and make a joyful celebration on a joyful human occasion.

In another instance, there was a man named Jairus, whose daughter died. Jesus went, raised her to life, and gave expression to an instant practical thought for her welfare when He commanded that she be given "meat"—something to eat.

Again, at the very end of His stay on earth, just before the Ascension into heaven, He saw the disciples fishing without success and told them where to cast their nets. The resulting catch was enormous. When they dragged it ashore, Jesus had a fire ready and gave the toil-weary fishermen a feast of broiled fish and bread, which he had evidently already prepared. This story, told in Saint John's Gospel, closely parallels in time and place the story told in Saint Luke's Gospel about the fish Jesus ate in order to convince the disciples that it really was their Master who stood before them in the Resurrected, if transformed, flesh.

If food and drink are elemental factors in human life, the dining table was also a very central aspect of Hebraic life in those days. It was the focal point of discourse and relaxation. It is therefore natural that Jesus should have interspersed references to food and drink and dining so often among His teachings, both direct and parabolic. He knew that besides the hunger in man's body there is the more hidden hunger in man's soul. Even before the first miracle of providing drink for the wedding guests, He had Himself experienced such hunger during his fast in the wilderness that He had laid Himself open to the Devil's tempting Him to make bread out of stones.

Early in His teaching ministry, He gave voice in the Sermon on the Mount to the importance of spiritual hunger and spiritual feeding. "Blessed" (happy), said Jesus, "are they which do hunger and thirst after righteousness: for they shall be filled." He was not saying that hunger itself is blessed, but only the great rewards of *hunger for righteousness*—"for they shall be filled" with righteousness.

This theme was to recur again and again. I would not for a moment suggest that Jesus overlooked the essential need of physical food. In teaching men how to pray, He did not fail to include a petition that the Father "give us this day our daily bread." He taught in the most forthright terms that it is our duty to love our fellow beings by feeding them when they are hungry: "For I was an hungered, and ye gave me meat: I was thirsty and ye gave me drink." And when the rather slow-witted disciples asked when they had ever seen Him hungry and fed Him, He gave the teaching a needle-sharp point: "inasmuch as ye have done it unto one of the least of these my brethren, ye have done it unto me" (Saint Matthew 25:40). Thus, at a stroke, Jesus established social concern as one of the chief duties of the individual Christian. He gave meaning to His Second Commandment: "Thou shalt love thy neighbor as thyself." Feed the hungry, was His clear command.

But it has always seemed to me that His greatest concern was with spiritual hunger. This was a frequent and central theme of His teachings. There is more to our existence than a stomach in a body. There is a greater goal than to keep body and soul together until tomorrow. That greater goal is to grow spiritually to know the peace of God, "which passeth under-standing." Only the man with a sharp spiritual hunger—and I suppose it is, alas, all too true that much of mankind seems to be unaware of that hunger—will be filled with the righteous-ness that leads to eternal life with God. This was distinctly *the* important hunger to Immanuel. He sprinkled His speech liberal-ly with references to it.

Perhaps the best example is found in the famous Scriptural passage considerably elaborated in the sixth chapter of Saint John's Gospel: "I am the bread of life; he that cometh to me shall never hunger; and he that believeth on me shall never thirst." Embroidering broadly on this theme, Jesus went on to make the point clear again in similar words: "I am the living bread which came down from heaven: if any man eat of this bread, he shall live for ever. . . . "

One might almost say that Jesus was obsessed with this motif of spiritual hunger and its satisfaction through Him. When He attended the Temple for the Feast of Tabernacles, He stood and cried aloud in the midst of the people and His enemies, "If any man thirst, let him come unto me and drink." His enemies, who sought to take Him, were put to confusion by this teaching. They spared Him temporarily, and His saying rings out across the centuries to us: "I am the bread of life." And the water.

The point made in public was also made in private. Consider that intriguing meeting at the well with the woman of Samaria. Casually (or was it by design?) Jesus sat by a well. A woman came to draw water, and He asked her for a drink. The conversation thus opened, He skillfully turned it to the subject of "living water" which He could give her. He told her that He was the very Messiah, the Christ, thus echoing Gabriel, who had announced Immanuel to Mary. The woman believed and spread the news abroad, and numerous conversions resulted. (See Saint John 4:5–30, 39–42.) When, at day's

54

end, the disciples urged him to eat, Jesus repeated the lesson by saying, "I have meat to eat of that ye know not of."

Can one doubt that this was Immanuel, "God with us," very God and very man? On the Cross itself, His human nature so tormented Him that He cried out in agony, "I thirst." However, after the Resurrection, almost the last command He gave to His disciples was concerned with the spiritual food that He alone could provide. Thrice He addressed to Peter the command: "Feed my sheep." Feed the bodily hungry with earthly food. Even more important, feed the spiritually hungry that they may have eternal life with God.

Notes

1. It must be noted, however, that Mark 2:1–2 indicates that Jesus may have had a home early in his ministry, in Capernaum.
2. With regard to the stories of the feeding of the five thousand and the four thousand, respectively, there is some confusion and debate. A common assumption is that these may have been two versions of one incident. But Mark 8:19–20 clearly indicates, on the face of it, that there were *two* feedings of the multitude.

12
Loving the Unlovable

As we go through life, we observe that the rich and the famous, the great and the learned, the successful and the leaders mostly associate with their equals. I cannot recall ever hearing of one of them who was in the habit of frequently talking or dining with the down-and-out, with criminals, with prostitutes, with garbage collectors and ditch diggers, with the socially unacceptable or even with socially acceptable enemies. Oh, we know that candidates for public office do go out and "press the flesh," shake hands, kiss babies, and otherwise "mingle" with all classes of the citizenry. But this is not done out of love and concern for the people. It is strictly a necessary vote-getting exercise.

Immanuel was different.

Through the entire life and message of Jesus runs the thread of compassion for the unfortunate, the despised, the downtrodden. The infinite value, the spiritual equality, of all men in the eyes and in the love of God is emphasized again and again. To illustrate these lessons, Jesus associated with, comforted, and forgave people who were beyond the pale in one way or another. Look at a few examples.

Jesus called Levi (Matthew) to be one of His disciples. Levi was a publican, a despised collector of taxes and therefore an extortioner. Worse still, Levi gathered together other publicans and gave a feast for Jesus. This caused an angry murmur among the scribes and Pharisees. They actually upbraided Jesus, asking Him why He so defied custom as to eat with such people. His answer was one that He was to give time and again—that He came to call sinners to repentance and that it is the sick who need the physician (Saint Luke 5:27–32).

Then there was the half-amusing, wholly-revealing incident with Zacchaeus. Zacchaeus was a publican, too, and he wanted to see this famous teacher, Jesus, when He came to the publican's hometown of Jericho. But Zacchaeus was a short man and he couldn't see over the heads of the people in the crowds. So he climbed a tree, and it was in this vantage place that the Lord saw him and promptly told him to come down and suggested that he take Him home as a guest. Again the protest arose, from the very proper leaders of society, that Jesus was the guest of a sinner. The answer this time was the same in substance, although different in words. He pointed out that this man, Zacchaeus, was also a son of Abraham like all the rest of them and therefore, by implication, no less dear to God. He said He had come to save the lost. To cap the climax, He forgave Zacchaeus his sins because he gave half of all he had to the poor (Saint Luke 19:2–10).

Prostitutes then, as now, though patronized, were treated with contempt and scorn, treated harshly when caught. Jesus was faced with such a scene where a prostitute was about to be stoned to death for her wrongdoing. He intervened. First He stooped and wrote something in the sand. (How devoured one is with curiosity to know what He wrote, but the Scriptures do not tell us.) Then He commanded the first stone to be thrown by anyone who had not sinned. No stones were thrown, the crowd melted away, shamed, and Jesus forgave the woman and told her not to sin again (Saint John 8:3–11). This incident certainly reveals the commanding presence and power of Immanuel, but more importantly it reveals His concern for the outcasts, the "untouchables," the sinners who have learned their lesson.

On another occasion, He accepted a Pharisee's invitation to dine. (Saint Luke 7:36–48 tells this story. Saint Matthew 26:6–13 tells of a very similar, if not the identical, incident, placing it at the home of a leper.) A woman of the town, "a sinner" and therefore probably a prostitute, followed Him into the house, and while He was at table she bathed His feet with an expensive perfumed oil or ointment and dried the feet with her long hair, weeping the while. The host, whose name was Simon, whether Pharisee or leper or both, muttered to himself in scorn that if this man were truly a prophet He would have known the woman for what she was and would not have allowed her to touch Him. Jesus knew his thoughts, read him a stern lecture on his lack of courteous hospitality as compared with the woman's generous devotion, and forgave her her sins.

One of the incidents most familiar to us happened at Sychar, in Samaria, when Jesus, weary from travel, sat down to rest on the edge of a famous well that had belonged to Jacob some eighteen hundred years before. A Samaritan woman approached to draw water, and He engaged her in conversation. No self-respecting Jew would have done this. First, she was a woman with whom he was unacquainted. Second, and far worse, she was a Samaritan, a race anathema to orthodox Jews. Third, as He soon discovered, she had had five husbands and was therefore an adulteress, a grievous sinner. But—and this "but" overrides all else—He also found that she had a deep spiritual thirst and a ready faith. He satisfied that thirst by telling her about the "living" water that He could provide to her. Many conversions resulted among the inhabitants of Sychar because of her faith. (See Saint John 4:5–42.) He might so easily have turned His back on this woman in sanctimonious righteousness. But He scorned legalistic and formalistic conventions and superficial self-righteousness. Where sin and need and ostracism were, there was He, teaching, loving, forgiving.

There is one more example of loving "the wrong people," and in some ways this is the most striking example of all. On Calvary, He hung nailed to the Cross, suffering agonies of pain. On either side of Him were crucified thieves, "malefactors," convicted criminals. One rebuked the other for taunting the dying Lord, who was an innocent man while they, the two malefactors, were guilty. Even in His agony, Christ saw here a child of God, a penitent sinner, and turned His head and promised him entrance into paradise (Saint Luke 23:33, 39–43). What a crystal clear manifestation of love for the unlovable, and at such a moment!

By these and other actions Jesus showed His deep and constant concern for those whom others classed as socially unacceptable, to be shunned. He reinforced His actions with words on many occasions. "When thou makest a feast," He told a Pharisee, "call the poor, the maimed, the lame, the blind . . . for thou shalt be recompensed at the resurrection at the last" (Saint Luke 14:13). Parable after parable proclaimed that the last shall be first, the lost will be found, the "least of these shall be ministered unto," and even "the publicans and the harlots" (Saint Matthew 21:31) shall enter the kingdom of God.

"Come unto me, all ye that labor and are heavy laden, and I will give you rest" (Saint Matthew 11:28). Thus Jesus summed up his doctrine of love and compassion, of concern and forgiveness, of equality in the sight of God.

These are hard lessons. They go absolutely contrary to the values and standards and mores of this world and our society. Still, it is marvelously reassuring to note how often this lesson *is* taken to heart and put into practice. We have only to think of the Red Cross and its work of succor to the down-and-out after disaster. We have only to think of the unimaginable self-giving of a Mother Teresa in Calcutta. We have only to think of the innumerable examples of loving concern for the sinners and the destitute, as typified by the work of devoted Christians at Covenant House in the sinkhole of the Times Square area of New York City and elsewhere.

Only recently I read of a poor black man in Virginia, whose retirement income was minuscule, who was buried in medical debts because of the illness of his wife and whose misfortunes were climaxed when the county attached his poor home to pay for garbage disposal service which he never used. The instant outpouring of help when this story was published must have gladdened the hearts of angels in heaven.

This is surely "God with us," Immanuel still residing in the hearts of men in the late twentieth century: "Inasmuch as ye have done it unto one of the least of these my brethren . . . " (Saint Matthew 25:40).

13
Setting the Goals

We rather come to the heart of the whole matter when we ask, what did this Jesus, this Messiah, this Immanuel, seek to accomplish? What were the lessons He sought to spread before all who would listen, whether in the world of Caesar Tiberius or in the world of 1991 or in the world of 9591, if it should last that long?

Before we can answer that question directly, there is a prior question to ask and answer, and the answer is virtually a giveaway of the answer to our main question. Why did God send his Son into this isolated corner of the cosmos? The answer to this preliminary question seems rather simple to me. God wanted mankind to have a closer sense of him, to know him better, and to realize the endless depths of his love for this creature, man. He wanted man to be able to walk in the light, and so he created light on the first day of creation; so Genesis tells us. But he also, and more fervently, wanted man to have a spiritual light to guide him, and so in due time he sent the co-existing Word, his Son, to be the "light that shineth in the darkness," as Saint John, the great spiritual understander of God, put it in the first chapter of his Gospel. In his good time, God sent that Word, that Light, into the world.

Love, light, and life were God's goals. They pretty well sum up the goals Immanuel set for Himself. How did He arrive at these goals? As we have already indicated, they probably evolved out of long and earnest meditation and study during His teens and twenties. Then, as we also saw, it is very likely that His goals were finally firmed up and the course of action necessary to attain them was fixed upon during His retreat into the wilderness and His encounter there with Satan.

Jesus' goal clearly was to bring to men some understanding of divine love, of the love of God for them, and of the love they should return to God and to their fellowmen. In this sense, the somewhat trite summation by some Christians that "God is love" is not incorrect. On the other hand, *love* is a word so loosely and variously used in modern society that we must take care to define it more closely. Nobody who takes Jesus seriously can suppose that He was talking of the eroticism which today so often passes as "love." Nor was He talking about even the natural and high-minded love of a man and a woman for each other that results in marriage. He also didn't have in mind even the trusting and giving love we feel for our parents and our children. Most certainly He wasn't thinking of the namby-pamby sentimentalism pictured as "love" in fiction and drama. It also seems quite clear that He meant for His followers to draw a distinction between liking and loving. He talked about "loving" our enemies and those who do us harm and evil. He did not say we should "like" such people, but that we should "love" them.

What is this strange love, this deific love that we should strive to emulate? Inasmuch as all things about God are essentially incomprehensible, the love of God is essentially incomprehensible. But perhaps what Jesus had in mind can be comprehended dimly if we start from His teaching that every human being is a creature of God, created by God, considered of value—that is, "loved"—by God. Therefore, the love which is Immanuel's goal for us is a respect for that spark of God which is in every human being, however thoroughly it may be buried or hidden. It is in even the vilest and worst among us. It is this respect for His divine origin that should enable us to hate the sin and "love" the sinner.

This message poured forth at the beginning of Immanuel's ministry, and it poured forth at the end. We see it first in the Sermon on the Mount, apparently preached soon after the forty days of fasting, meditation, temptation, and prayer in the desert place. Love between God and man is implicit in the Beatitudes and implicit in the many admonitions in the Sermon to righteousness of life and justness of attitude toward others. It is explicit in what I think of as the hard law of love, the command to "love your enemies," and in the admonition to "judge not, that ye be not judged." And it is recorded, by way of footnote to the thesis that Jesus was Immanuel and not a mere prophet, that "the people were astonished at his doctrine: For he taught them as one having authority, and not as the scribes." (See Saint Matthew 5–7.)

Then, at the very end of His ministry, Jesus reverted again to this basic theme when (as recorded in Chapters 13–17 of the Gospel of Saint John) He said to the Twelve, "This is my commandment, that ye love one another." In fact, He said it no fewer than three times on this one occasion. And He confirmed that this was the Father's purpose in sending Him into the world: "He that hath seen me hath seen the Father." In His final prayer on this last occasion of converse with His Apostles before His Resurrection, a prayer of such intensity that one trembles at the vibrations even when one reads it in cold print two thousand years later, He prayed, "And I have declared unto them thy name, and will declare it: that the love wherewith thou hast loved me may be in them, and I in them" (Saint John 17:26).

In between these two teachings are countless others, sometimes direct admonitions, sometimes more subtly expressed in parables and stories. We recall the parable of the mote one sees in the brother's eye while ignoring the beam in one's own eye. We recall the compassion and love that found expression so often in miracles of healing and raising from death and providing food or comfort to the hungry and distressed. We recall the parable of the man beset by thieves and succored by the good Samaritan. We recall the many admonitions to give alms and feed the poor. We recall the lesson about being first reconciled with your brother, if differences exist between you, before you go to the altar of God.

Again and again, Jesus exhorted His disciples, and His hearers generally, both followers and enemies, to do good, to *be* good, not to rely on legality, on observance of the letter of the Law alone, and on outward forms of piety, on fasting and breast-beating. Over and over, His teachings reflected and interpreted those of the Old Testament; Micah 6:8 comes to mind: "He hath shewed thee, O man, what is good; and what doth the Lord require of thee but to do justly, and to love mercy, and to walk humbly with thy God?" This kind of Old Testament teaching formed the core of Jesus' message. He was consumed with eagerness to reveal God to man, to show something of God's boundless love toward those who accept him, who love him, and who try to the best of their poor human ability to follow God's commandments.

Finally, in one supreme effort to make His point clear, Immanuel summarized His teachings in unmistakably plain and concise terms. "Thou shalt love the Lord thy God," Jesus said, "with all thy heart, and with all thy soul, and with all thy mind. This is the first and great commandment. And the second is like unto it, Thou shalt love thy neighbor as thyself." Then, to underscore the supreme importance of what He had said, He added, "On these two commandments hang all the law and the prophets," meaning that your worship, your whole understanding and practice of your religion, your whole comprehension of the teachings of the Old Testament and the Church, the entire way you live, all your attitudes and actions, shall all be governed by what He had just set forth in these two commands. (See Saint Matthew 22:37–40.)

Thus did Immanuel set forth His goal, which was to teach divine love, and thus did He set forth our goal, to practice divine love as far as in us lies.

14

Laying Hypocrisy Bare

Most of what Jesus did and said was couched in positive terms. His thrust was constructive. He healed. He helped. He commanded positive acts such as "love thy neighbor." Of course there were some of the negative "don'ts" with a flavor of the Old Testament, such as "go and sin no more." For the most part, however, His life and message were of the upbeat kind.

There is one glaring exception. It concerns hypocrisy. On this subject He spoke often and usually harshly and scathingly. God is pure and positive. Immanuel was pure and positive. He simply could not tolerate pretense and subterfuge and insincerity, and hypocrisy is compounded of just such elements.

The hypocrite pretends to be what he is not—good when he is bad, just when he is unjust, the model of pious rectitude when he is in fact an impious scoundrel. The hypocrite pretends.

Accused, the hypocrite says, "Who, *me*? How can you accuse me of false dealings when you know I attend church, drop pennies in the beggar's hand, and lend my name to every good cause?" The hypocrite likes to make excuses, to hide behind elaborate and lovely stage settings. The hypocrite is a master of subterfuge.

The hypocrite says one thing and means another. "I believe in God," he says, "and I keep his laws." In fact, what he believes in and keeps are not the Ten Commandments, but the laws of custom and ritual and procedure with which man has surrounded the laws of God. The hypocrite skitters over the surface of life, behavior, and worship, trusting to appearances to mask the real self that often he himself does not realize lies within. Honest sincerity does not dwell in the hypocrite.

Immanuel could not stand this. It offended Him grievously. Sin, open sin, acknowledged sin, He could tolerate and forgive. It was to repentant sinners that He could gently turn with loving admonition to stop their sin and start afresh.

Toward hypocrites He was scathing. Sometimes His wrath was expressed in general terms. The sixth chapter of Saint Luke's Gospel provides examples: Don't give alms with a flourish of trumpets. Don't make a great public show of prayer, as much as to say with little Jack Horner, "What a good boy am I"! Don't put on a long, haggard face when you fast, as if to say, "See how dutifully I suffer from my religious exercises!" It is true that these were negative "don'ts," but they were always followed by positive "do's." Give alms quietly, even confidentially when you can. Fast in the sight of God, with a glad and unworried face. Let your prayers be modest, even in the secrecy of your heart. Incidentally, this last cannot be read as condemning common prayer in public services, for Jesus Himself attended the synagogue and Temple services. What He did condemn was the ostentatious "for show" praying of the Pharisee in the Temple.

There were other such examples. When He was asked why His disciples did not always perform the ritual washing of the hands before eating, He rejoined to the sticklers for ritual who questioned Him that they were the very hypocrites whom Elijah had condemned as honoring God with their lips while despising him with their hearts because, as Elijah added, they obey men's regulations instead of God's laws.

And again, Jesus spoke of the ease and certainty with which men could read the weather from the sky and the wind, but how impossible it seemed for them to look within themselves and judge honestly of what they saw there.

The full fury of Jesus' attack against hypocrisy comes out in that terrible twenty-third chapter of Saint Matthew's Gospel. Here He pulled no punches. Here, in a relatively rare exhibition of wrathful indignation, He named not only the sins of hypocrisy, but the practitioners of hypocrisy. He gave the scribes and the Pharisees a black name and a tongue-lashing from which their reputation has never recovered. Eight times, in a succession of pile-driving blows, He said, "Woe unto you, scribes and Pharisees, hypocrites." In seven different figures of speech He pounded home the message.

He accused these hypocrites of prating about heaven but blocking the door to it for those who would enter by insisting on observance of every single ritualistic provision of the Law rather than upon compliance with the substance of faith. He castigated them for defrauding widows while praying virtuously. He condemned them for seeking converts only in order to mold them into their own hypocritical type. He denounced them for swearing by—taking their stand on—secondary incidentals, not the primary essentials of their religious faith. He rebuked them for paying their tithes meticulously but neglecting to be just, merciful, and faithful. In two different figures of speech He berated them for keeping up virtuous appearances on the outside, while letting what is inside rot in filth. He indicted them for honoring the prophets (and simultaneously honoring their forefathers) while saying they themselves would never have treated the prophets so badly, masking the fact that it was their own forefathers who killed the prophets.

Christ called hypocrisy the yeast which leavened and shaped the lives of the Pharisees. He predicted it would always be found out. He pronounced that the man who lived by hypocrisy and thus disowned God (Immanuel) would hereafter be disowned in the presence of God's angels. The hypocrite would not escape until the very last penny of his debt, his punishment, was paid.

Jesus' attack on the Pharisees was as terrible as any attack He ever launched. Yet of course we must take note of the fact that He attacked them not because they were Pharisees, but because they were such conspicuous hypocrites. The falseness of hypocrisy simply could not coexist with the two great Commandments He once summarized—love God and love your fellowman. One cannot suppose for a moment that He condemned all Pharisees indiscriminately. That would have been contrary to His whole spirit. One remembers, and I will have occasion later to speak of him again, the good Pharisee, Nicodemus, no hypocrite, no "yes-man," but an earnest seeker after the truth.

No, it was not a class but a condition that Jesus attacked time and again. God praised Ezekiel as a wise man and said, "there is no secret that they can hide from thee" (Ezekiel 28:3). How much wiser is God than Ezekiel, and how impossibly absurd and wicked it is to try to hide secrets from him under spurious outward trappings of virtue. It is so absurd that it angered Immanuel to the very core of His being. God cannot be fooled, wherever he is or whatever his form.

15

"Whom Do Men Say That I Am?"[1]

There was a pregnant encounter between Jesus and His disciples at some point probably well along in His ministry. Three of the Evangelists, Matthew, Mark and John, all record that on one occasion the Lord turned to His closest followers and put a blunt and rather strange question to them: "Whom do men say that I the Son of Man am?" (I quote Saint Matthew's language, 16:13.) They replied that He was variously thought to be John the Baptist or one of the great prophets of the Old Testament.

Then, without comment on this answer as far as the record shows, He asked straight out, "But whom say *ye* that I am?" (emphasis mine). With equal directness came the answer from Peter, the spokesman for them all: "Thou art the Christ, the Son of the living God." The Master accepted this without denial, but He at once called Peter "blessed."

What does this incident mean, this cameolike moment of give-and-take with the Twelve? Was Jesus seeking reassurance about Himself and His mission? Was He unaware of His identity? Was He having second thoughts, a moment of doubt about His true nature? Not at all, by the cumulative evidence of the record. We have seen Him already at the early age of twelve speaking of His father, obviously not meaning Joseph. He had heard God's voice at Jordan and seen the dove descend on Himself. He had wrestled successfully with the wily Devil, He had turned water into wine, He had healed the sick and lame and blind, He had fed the five thousand, and He had raised the dead to life. He *knew* who He was; He was in no uncertainty whatever.

In asking these questions, it seems to me, He was after what we might call a status report. What had been the effect of His teachings and His miracles? What kind of impression had He made on the people generally and, far more important, how did His special followers regard Him by now? The chronology is so uncertain that we cannot be sure whether He had ever up to this time made a specific claim to be God as well as man. He was apparently in the habit of regularly referring to Himself as "the Son of Man." To insist too openly, too quickly, upon His other, divine, nature would have been to claim the unbelievable, to create a possibly unbridgeable gap between Him and His followers. He had first to establish his authority as a human teacher and then step by step to lead His disciples to a recognition of His deity.

So, by degrees, He had let His full nature reveal itself. He often spoke of "the Father," of "him who sent me," of "the Kingdom of Heaven." He had opened successive shutters, little by little. He had performed marvellous acts which helped establish His fame. He had trusted to these acts and His teachings and the perfect character which He constantly revealed to establish His true nature. Now came confirmation that His hope, His plan, His program had succeeded. He was hailed by Peter on behalf of the disciples as "Son of the living God."

This ripening of recognition is spread out for us to see. Several years earlier, at the start of the Galilean ministry, Andrew had exclaimed to his brother Peter (one can almost hear the breathlessness!), "We have found the Messias [Messiah]" (Saint John 1:41). A little later on a certain occasion, Peter himself had fallen on his knees before Jesus and called him "Lord" (Saint Luke 5:8). Still later, Peter had said, " . . . we

71

. . . are sure that thou art that Christ, the Holy one of God" (as most translations put it—Saint John 6:69).

Little by little, recognition of this man's true identity had burgeoned in the disciples. Now it came forth in full blossom with Peter's answer to the Lord's question: "Whom say ye that I am?"—"Thou art the Christ, the Son of the living God." Some of the previous recognition had burst out in impetuous emotional reaction to some act or word of Christ's. Peter's words now seem to be the response of a more studied, deeper conviction, a direct answer to a direct question. It represented full recognition at last.

It is possible, and perhaps necessary, to say that Peter's testimony on this occasion represented intellectual recognition, not yet the full recognition of faith. Acceptance by the mind and acceptance by faith are two different levels of acceptance, and who is to say that recognition by faith is not the higher level? There were, of course, to be many backslidings from this recognition before the final triumph of faith. There were to be Peter's denials, thrice repeated, in the palace of the high priest; there was to be Judas's irrevocable betrayal; there was to be the absence of every one of the Twelve save John at the Crucifixion; there were the doubts after the Resurrection, summed up and immortalized in Thomas's demand to see the physical evidence.

Nevertheless, at the moment of Jesus' question and Peter's answer the Lord must have been well content. The chosen followers were clearly beginning to know and accept Him as Immanuel.

Note

1. I quote the exact language of the KJV here. The learned translators sadly slipped when they used the accusative "whom" instead of the nominative "who"—or was English grammar simply more imprecise and unformed in the seventeenth century than now?

16

Foreglimpse of Heaven

A very strange thing indeed happened to Immanuel about halfway through His ministry. The Gospel writers were not too concerned about the particulars of chronology, but it would appear that this strange event took place fairly soon after the feeding of the five thousand. But no matter. It is not the timing that is important but rather the significance of what actually occurred.

The story is told in very similar terms by Saints Matthew, Mark, and Luke and is indirectly adverted to by Saint John and by Saint Peter. It seems that one day Jesus took the three disciples who were closest to Him and who, He thought, had made the greatest strides in understanding Him—Peter, James, and John—and led them up onto the slopes of a high mountain or hill. Some scholars think the height was Mount Hermon; He had been in nearby Caesarea Philippi only a few days before, by all the evidence. This kind of withdrawal into a wild, unsettled area was a rather common practice of the Master whenever the pressures of the crowd and His ministry began to weigh rather heavily upon Him. No doubt the three disciples thought they were again going apart solely for a session of prayer and instruction.

What actually took place, however, was so different and so startling that the three lost their moorings altogether. They seem never to have spoken of that day's events for a long time to come, perhaps fearing they would be laughed to scorn. At some future time they do appear to have talked about it, probably after the Ascension and/or Pentecost, because Saints Matthew, Mark, and Luke knew and wrote about it in some detail.

The astonishing sequence of events was this. Jesus and the others did actually pray, just as the disciples had anticipated. However, as Christ prayed, His appearance was startlingly altered. It is hard to say just what happened. The Gospel accounts strike me as being at a loss for appropriate descriptive words. They all speak in terms of shining light and absolutely dazzling whiteness, so that the three apparently could scarcely look upon their Master. They compared the light to that of the sun, and the whiteness of His garments was described as "glistering" (how often have you seen anything you would describe with that word?), white as snow, whiter than any bleach could make cloth.

Then, suddenly, the three witnesses saw that He talked with two men, who were Moses and Elijah. It has always intrigued me to speculate as to how they knew the identities of the strangers; of course, they did not wear identifying name tags, nor does anyone seem to have introduced them! But God has his own way of creating recognition. Apparently the conversation was loud enough and real enough that the three disciples distinctly heard talk of their Master's coming death in Jerusalem.

Faced with this scene, Peter, in his usual impulsive way, said the first thing that came into his mind, which in this case appears rather ludicrous in retrospect. He proposed that three huts or tents be set up so that Jesus and the prophets could talk in comfort, shielded from the hot sun—or possibly his object was to commemorate the occasion by erecting three rude memorial shelters. At any rate, Jesus is not recorded as having reacted to Peter's suggestion. The Gospels record it but then consign it to discreet silence, so apparently nothing came of it.

After a bit—the details are a trifle sketchy and disordered—a "cloud" wrapped itself around the summit where they were. The disciples were uneasy to the point of fear, and especially when a voice came out of the cloud and proclaimed that "this is my beloved Son; hear him." When the cloud was past, Jesus was alone again. He reassured the frightened three, bade them keep these happenings a secret, and they all went back down the mountain.

This was decidedly not your everyday, run-of-the-mill experience in life. It has always appeared to me that one reason why the disciples obeyed the Lord's injunction to keep silence was simply because they themselves could make neither head nor tail of what they had seen until long afterward. Through most of my life I certainly made little sense of it. No minister or book crossing my path ever said much about it, and certainly nothing that impressed me as making much sense. Moreover, even in liturgical churches the day particularly dedicated to remembering this event is little noticed because it falls on a set day (August 6) and therefore coincides with Sunday church services but seldom.

Mature reflection in later life (possibly spurred on by reading a chapter in that wonderful book *The Lord*, by Romano Guardini) has given me what are, at any rate to me, some satisfying insights into what is known as the Transfiguration. It was obviously intended to be part of the education of the three disciples, but this is bound to have been only an incidental purpose. It was a revelation for, to, and through Jesus of His nature and of His future. It was a further imprimatur of God's favor. It was a confirmation of the voice at the Jordan baptism. It was a tremendous and supernatural revelation in space and time of Christ's oneness with the Godhead. In its way, it was a preliminary rehearsal of the tremendous force that wrested victory from death in the tomb. It was a rehearsal for the Resurrection.

Its significance was too great for the disciples to grasp at that stage. It was too far outside their experience to be comprehended. What mere man could possibly understand a sudden irradiation transforming a rabbi, a teacher, a friend, a Master, into a being so shining as to be indescribable, so transformed as to be almost unbearable to look upon? What mere man could understand the sudden visible presence of long-gone men and servants of God such as Moses and Elijah? What mere man could hear without abject quaking a voice from nothingness, from a nothingness so impenetrable as only to be described as a cloud, the terrible, loving, majestic, overriding voice of God? They must indeed have tottered down the mountain like sleepwalkers, on very shaky legs!

Frozen in time, incomprehensible in this world's terms, this mountaintop happening cannot be dismissed as the hallucination of three disordered and preconditioned minds. No, it was a sign to Christ of His forthcoming victory, an assurance in advance that His suffering would not be in vain. It was deity, urgent and irresistible, breaking for a moment through the bonds of mortality, the confining restraints of human nature. Years later, the three witnesses recognized it for what it was, Immanuel in glory. "We beheld His glory," wrote Saint John, "the glory as of the only begotten of the Father" (Saint John 1:14). And Saint Peter added that "we were eyewitnesses of his majesty" (II Peter 1:16).

17

A Farewell Dinner

It is a common custom among us to honor someone who is approaching the end of a period of important service with a farewell dinner, usually a brilliant affair of some pomp and ceremony. The approaching end of Immanuel's earthly career was marked by a dinner, too, but it was far from the kind of laudatory and lionizing celebration we are used to. In this case, the honoree was the host, the meal was simple, the guests were but twelve in number, and the only speech was a brief but striking one by the host.

It came about in this way (and Saints Matthew, Mark, and Luke tell the story in almost the same words). Jesus and His disciples came up to Jerusalem to celebrate the Passover, that great feast commemorating the way in which the angel of death had smitten the Egyptians back in Moses' time but had spared, "passed over," the Hebrews. The account of the place of the group's celebration is very curious. The disciples asked where they would have the Passover meal. Jesus told two of them to go into the city until they saw a man carrying a pitcher of water—unusual in itself, because it was women who normally drew and carried water. The two were to follow this man to his house and then say to him that "the Master" asks where the room is where He would eat the Passover meal. The man would then show them a large upstairs room, and they should prepare that room for the meal. Thus, in this curious and inexplicable fashion, it was done. What was at work here? Prearrangement? Telepathy? Who was the strange "goodman" of the house? We do not know.

Thus it was that the Twelve and the One sat down or reclined at the table together. We have always pictured it as either a long table or a U-shaped table with Jesus at the center. That would be appropriate, and perhaps it was so. We do know from the scriptural account that John sat next to the Lord. How the others were arranged is unknown and unimportant. The table was furnished with wine and the traditional unleavened bread; if there was anything else, it is not mentioned. Jesus, as host and Master, took charge. He said a grace, a prayer of thanksgiving, before distributing the bread. Then He made a curious statement, seemingly without explanation. He said that the bread was His body, "given for you," and that they should eat it in remembrance of Him. Then He did the same with the wine, saying it was His blood, shed for many "for the remission of sins." The ceremony was very simple, but it must have perplexed the Twelve no end at the time. Nevertheless, they never forgot exactly what was said and done. Like so many other actions and sayings which made no sense to them at the time, this ceremony made crystal-clear sense to them after the Resurrection, the Ascension, and the descent of the Holy Ghost at Pentecost. They, and those who came after them in the Faith, followed the commands given by the Lord at the Passover table, followed them faithfully and permanently, knowing at last full well who Jesus was and what He meant by His body given for them and His blood spilled for them and for many.

Thus took place the central act of that first Maundy Thursday, the day of the Lord's mandate or command. How the memory of that last intimate, mysterious supper with Immanuel must have haunted the disciples—at first with perplexity and later with comforting reassurance. How closely at one with Him they must have felt throughout the rest of their lives each time they partook of His broken body and His shed blood!

Several other things happened at that supper which greatly intrigue my imagination. First, not only in the words already quoted but also more explicitly, He told them (and not for the first time) of His coming death. Almost certainly, they didn't really take in the literal meaning of His words. They are not quoted as having protested, "No, no, Lord," or as having asked questions. However, two of them got involved in the discussion in spite of themselves.

Peter, ever forward and prompt of speech, protested that however much other men might accuse and attack Jesus, he, Peter, would never join them; rather, he would go with his Master either to prison or to death. Then Jesus, with the insight into coming events that He so often displayed, told Peter that he would "deny" Him, disclaim Him, disavow Him, three times before the next day broke. Peter was aghast, even angry, at this aspersion on his loyalty and courage and vehemently asserted again that he would stick by Jesus through thick and thin; in this avowal all the others (including Judas, one wonders?) joined Peter. There the record drops the story, but what astonishment and stir it must have caused in the ranks— perhaps even resentment that their faithfulness under stress could be doubted. Next morning, after his third denial that he ever knew Jesus, Peter was to remember and he "wept bitterly." One wonders whether the other disciples (except for John), who seem to have been too timid and afraid to be present even as silent followers at the Crucifixion, also remembered and wept bitterly.

Then there was Judas. Among other remarks concerning His approaching death, Jesus said that one person at the table would betray Him, but He named no name. The table was thrown into an uproar, each man asking the others and asking

Jesus who this could be and whether it might be he himself. Saint Matthew even asserts that Judas explicitly asked the Lord if it was he (from the scriptural account one understands that he had already agreed with the chief priests to betray his Master) and the Lord explicitly said that it *was* he (Saint Matthew 26:25). I take the liberty of doubting this particular question and answer, which are given only by Saint Matthew, because it may be supposed that the specific accusation against Judas would have caused a storm of indignation, maybe even bodily punishment, to have broken over Judas from his fellows. What this exchange surely does reveal, however, is the inner agony of conscience and turmoil of shame that must have overcome the disciple from Kerioth at that moment. The turmoil was so great that the traitor did hang himself afterwards. Perhaps it would have been better if on that Thursday evening he had gotten up from the table and gone out and hanged himself then and there. But just as God would have found another way if Mary had refused the Archangel Gabriel's request, so he would have found another way even if Judas had not gone through with his treasonable role later that night.

Thus the story of Immanuel rolled on towards its conclusion, in a quiet upper-story room at an intimate supper on that Thursday Passover evening. Jesus predicted a desertion and a betrayal—and what pain this must have caused Him, because what is worse than to be deserted or betrayed by those who have been closest to you in a great cause? In spite of this pain and disappointment, He bequeathed to His followers an act whereby they could be united with Him again and again through the ages to come and in the process gain strength to be His witnesses in faith and action.

And afterward they sang a hymn—how I would like to know what the words of the hymn were[1]—and went out to the

Mount of Olives for Immanuel's last moments of human freedom.

Note

1. If the Last Supper was indeed the Passover supper, as Saints Matthew, Mark, and Luke (but not John) indicate, then the "hymn" may have been the ritual singing of Psalms 115–118, four great songs of praise.

18
Accepting the Inevitable

Everything we say and think about Immanuel has to be based on the fact that this amalgam of God and man is essentially inexplicable and incomprehensible in human terms, to the human mind. All explanations, all suppositions, are limited by this fact. Apart from the written record of what He said and what He did, all our attempts to penetrate beneath the surface are sheer guesswork. God told Moses that he could not look upon him and live, nor could any man (Exodus 33:20). Saint John passes on to us the same message: "No man hath seen God at any time" (Saint John 1:18). He is invisible to the human eye. He is also invisible to the human mind, which can never penetrate the cloud that surrounds God—surrounded him when he spoke with Moses on Mount Sinai, surrounded him when Solomon dedicated the Temple, surrounded him on the Mount of Transfiguration. Recognizing this, the Athanasian Creed sums it up in three staccato phrases: "the Father incomprehensible, the Son incomprehensible: and the Holy Ghost incomprehensible." This incomprehensibility of God in all his aspects must perforce always underlie our approaches to God.

Because we cannot see God, nor comprehend him, we cannot really get very far into the mind of Immanuel. We do not know at what point He understood fully the fate that was in store for Him as a human being. We do not know at what point He grappled with the knowledge of this fate and accepted it as the will of the Father. But accept it Immanuel did. The record makes that quite clear.

It is fruitless to speculate about the degree and time of His self-knowledge, whether He knew about his coming sacrifice from childhood or whether it became apparent to Him only as His ministry progressed. At some point, He began talking about His coming death. The first recorded instance seems to have been shortly after the feeding of the five thousand, when He told the disciples that He would be slain. They didn't understand, persisting in their blindness to the day of Crucifixion itself.

Again, at the Transfiguration, the three disciples with Him heard Moses and Elijah conversing with the Lord about His approaching decease. Again the subject seems to have passed over their heads and was perhaps forgotten altogether at the moment in face of the stupefaction created by their inexplicable experience there on the Mount. The whole band of His disciples had another clear warning the very next day when their Master told them, slightly less explicitly, that "the Son of Man shall be delivered into the hands of men." Saint Luke (9:45) is quite explicit in telling us that the disciples did not understand this remark. On His final journey to Jerusalem, Jesus sought once more to tell them what lay ahead. The Gentiles would take Him, flog Him severely, and put Him to death. He also added, as He usually did, that He would rise again on the third day. Once more, His followers were completely mystified by such talk. Through Peter, they had already acknowledged Him as "the Christ, the Son of the living God," but this recognition was apparently so flawed, so imperfect, that they still could not wholly escape from their original picture of Him as a king coming into His kingdom, so how could a king be killed?

These blunt, direct statements about His death were

reinforced by many more obscure and indirect references. He had said that "this temple," meaning His body, would be destroyed and raised again in three days (Saint John 2:19). His hearers naturally thought He referred to Herod's Temple. Then, at the very end, at the Last Supper, He referred to His body as "broken" for them and His blood as shed for them and for many. No doubt such puzzling statements raised questions in their minds, but the subtlety was too great for them and clarity came only *post factum*.

These examples show clearly that Jesus had rather precise foreknowledge of the terrible agony that awaited Him and had it fairly early on, to say the least. Indeed, Saint John, with a keen spiritual perception *and* the benefit of hindsight, tells us straight out that Jesus knew "all things that should come upon him" (18:4). Yet it is also true that in spite of these clear and apparently calm predictions of what was to befall Him, there remained a corner of Jesus' mind which didn't really accept the absolute inevitability of his coming violent death.

The Last Supper being finished, the company went out towards the Mount of Olives. When they reached a place called Gethsemane, Jesus bade the main group of disciples to remain and pray while He went on a bit farther with Peter, James, and John, the three who seem to have had such a special relationship with Him. He then bade the three of them in turn to stay and watch. He Himself went a space apart and knelt down to pray. He begged His Father in heaven to "take away this cup from me" but added His submission to God's will, whatever that might be. Three times He wrestled thus with Himself and with His Father, always in the same words (Saint Matthew 26:39–44). His agony of inner despair and turbulence was so great that He burst into a violent perspiration. Perhaps blood vessels in His forehead broke, because the perspiration is described by Saint Luke as being like great drops of blood falling to the ground (Saint Luke 22:44). What profound spiritual agony is revealed in the pathos of this scene as Jesus struggled to accept His fate! An angel, by one account, appeared to comfort and strengthen Him, and one would gather from the nature of His prayer, from the inner agony, and finally by the presence of an angel that His acceptance was complete.

It is to be noted almost as a footnote to this tragic vignette, that three times He returned to the disciples, each time to find them sleeping. I have to confess that I almost feel outrage against them, that they could seem so indifferent to the fate and spirit of Jesus after such an evening of supper and prayer together. How *could* they be so apathetic, so unconcerned, as to leave their Master spiritually alone in His suffering at such a moment? Of course, the answer again is that they simply did not understand anything of what He had repeatedly told them, including His disturbing remarks at table in the Upper Room. Their human torpor and lack of discernment only underline His divine understanding and bring into sharp relief the tremendous change that came over them once the story was completed and the Holy Ghost came down upon them.

Thus, by stages, Jesus accepted the inevitable. Or did He absolutely and completely accept it? There was yet to come that final scene on the Cross. Having hung there for six hours, He suddenly cried out in the greatest of anguish, "My God, my God, why hast thou forsaken me?" If he felt Himself forsaken, perhaps this indicates that up to the very end there was in Him a tiny spark of resistance to what was happening, a tiny remnant of unwillingness to accept the inevitable. If this is indeed so, it was simply a last indication that Jesus' humanity, protesting, was still struggling against Immanuel's divinity, accepting. What a mirror of the struggle man puts up against accepting Immanuel!

19

Tragedy: Betrayed, Reviled, Condemned

Having accepted in prayer and agony in the Garden of Gethsemane the cruel human fate that awaited Him, Jesus turned to meet the approaching Judas. This Judas is properly the object of both contempt and pity. He is also something of a riddle. Here was a man who had been an intimate follower for three years. How was it possible that he could have so far escaped the beneficent magnetism and influence of his master as finally to turn against Him? Here was a man who only several hours before had heard his coming treachery predicted and who only a short time ago must have sneaked away from the sleeping disciples and gone to rendezvous with the authorities.

I have always wondered how such a weakling could have had the courage, or the nerve, to face either Jesus or the eleven who had hitherto been his fellows. The subsequent behavior of the other disciples is also puzzling. Several of them were armed, and when their Master was threatened with arrest one of them lashed out and cut off the ear of a servant of the high priest, one of the men who had come to seize Jesus. (The ear, incidentally, was promptly restored to its proper place, a last example of Christ's miraculous power of healing and also of His great compassion.) Why did no one turn on Judas, the promoter and agent of this betrayal? One would have thought their rage against this traitor would have been instantaneous and violent. But the record gives no indication of any such reaction, not even of verbal remonstrance.

The agreed-upon sign was given—that false and infamous kiss—and Jesus was arrested and taken off to the house of the high priest. There began His torment. He was blindfolded and struck in the face and mockingly told to use His miraculous power to say who had struck Him. One can see the ring of cruel, taunting, grinning faces as this game went on. At daybreak, the chief priests and other authorities questioned Him, seeking to trap Him into saying something they could use for their case against Him. They asked Him, for example, whether He was the Christ; He replied, in effect that there was no use in His answering the question, inasmuch as they wouldn't believe Him no matter what response He might give.

Then came the famous question: "Art thou then the Son of God?" It is a little hard to be absolutely sure what the answer was. Saints Matthew and Luke record the answer, according to the Authorized Version, as being in the somewhat cryptic form: "Thou hast said, " or "Ye say that I am." The Jerusalem Bible records the answer slightly differently as "the words are your own" or "it is you who say that I am." These answers are somewhat obscure and might mean "that's what you say; I haven't said so," or be taken as an affirmative answer.

In any case, however, He went on to assert that He would sit on the right hand of God and come in the "clouds of Heaven" (Saint Mark 14:62), clouds being the traditional symbol of the presence of God. All in all, considering Saint Mark's account that Jesus answered with a straightforward "I am," the preponderence of evidence seems to show that here Jesus directly claimed to be Immanuel. In so doing, He sealed His fate, for He laid Himself open to the charge of blasphemy, which could carry the death penalty.

Whether this cross-examination and abuse took place at night or only in the morning is uncertain, for the accounts are contradictory. But all agree that after daybreak the Council sent Him in fetters to Pontius Pilate, the Roman Governor, and demanded that He be put to death. In the process of transferral to Pilate, Jesus was pushed and shoved, slapped, spit upon, and subjected to contemptuous indignities. Pilate then questioned Jesus, getting mostly silence for a reply. Baffled, he decided to try to shift the responsibility over onto Herod, because Jesus was a Galilean and Herod, ruler of Galilee, happened to be in Jerusalem at that very time.

Herod himself was very glad to have Jesus brought before him because, according to Saint Luke, he was very curious to meet this man about whom he had heard so much. (Did he remember the story of his father's slaughter of the babies some thirty years earlier?) Herod Antipas's curiosity may have been tinged with just a touch of admiration. Those around Herod were, of course, bitter foes of Jesus. Herod asked many questions but, for whatever reasons, Jesus chose to answer nothing and to remain silent. This finally infuriated Herod and the Court and they subjected the Lord to renewed mockery and ridicule, finally sending Him back to Pilate in contemptuously-donated rich royal robes.

It is perhaps worth a moment of speculation as to why our Lord chose to remain utterly silent before Herod. One might suppose that He could possibly have seized here a small opportunity—not very hopeful, but an opening—to convince Herod of His true nature and intentions, given the ruler's eager curiosity. He chose the course of silence instead. Probably He recognized that, in the end, surrounded as the tetrarch was by Christ's enemies—"the chief priests and scribes"—the result would have been the same. Perhaps, too, He had retreated into some deep inner solitude of personal preparation for what was to come, a solitude so deep that He was scarcely aware by now of the world and the people around Him. No doubt this inner solitude protected and insulated His prayer communication with the Father, which must have been constant and indescribably intense.

Back before Pilate, He awaited sentence. Pilate seems to have been a man whose instincts were right and just. He didn't really think there was sufficient evidence to convict Jesus, let alone condemn Him to death. To reinforce this innate sense of justice, Pilate's wife sent him a message at this critical juncture, saying she had had a dream about Jesus and that Pilate should avoid judgment on "that just man." But it was all to no avail. A combination of the politics of the situation from Rome's point of view, pressure from the leaders of the Jewish Church, pressure from the large mob which had gathered, and, perhaps worst of all, some innate weakness or timidity in Pilate's character determined him to yield. Saint John directs a shaft of light into the inner working of Pilate's mind when he reports (19:12) that "the Jews" cried out to Pilate that he would be no friend of Caesar's if he released this man, because Caesar could not tolerate self-proclamations of kingship such as Jesus was accused of having made. This was a clever, and perhaps the decisive, ploy to bring Pilate around, for it implied talebearing to Caesar which might really rebound against him, Pilate, back in Rome.

Pilate had tried. Several times he had offered to release Jesus, in accordance with the custom of releasing a prisoner on the occasions of the high Jewish festivals. But the mob, prompted perhaps by the presence in its midst of agents provocateurs sent by the priests and scribes, demanded repeatedly that Jesus be crucified and that one Barabbas, variously described as a robber, an inciter to riot, and a murderer, should be released instead. Under all these pressures, Pilate yielded and gave Jesus up to be put to death by crucifixion. Who can say that any other man would have done better than Pilate under the circumstances?

The ritual whipping, which always followed a sentence of death, then occurred. There were a few embellishments, whether before or after judgment is not entirely clear. A crown was plaited of thorns (one hopes with unchristian vehemence that at least the plaiters got their fingers well pricked in the process!). A robe of royal purple was temporarily put on Jesus in mockery of His claim to be King of the Jews. He was at last led away, bearing (according to Saint John 19:17) His immensely heavy Cross toward the place called Golgotha or Calvary. (Saints Matthew, Mark, and Luke say that one Simon the Cyrenean was singled out of the crowd and compelled to shoulder the Cross.)

Several things about this whole episode give rise to speculation. I have always been struck by the sharp contrast between the enthusiastic crowds which had greeted Jesus' triumphal entry into Jerusalem less than a week before and the vengeful, vindictive mob which howled down Pilate's efforts to save Jesus on the fateful Friday. Was there some sudden violent swing in public opinion? Probably not. A poll in the current American fashion would probably have revealed that He still had wide popular backing. Perhaps some supporters had fallen away under the influence of the awful charges that this man Jesus was disloyal to the national religion and that He blasphemously claimed to be the Son of God. Then too, the Jews had been steeped in the belief that a warlike king would come to lead them. The man who had ridden into Jerusalem on an ass and the man who seemingly tamely submitted to arrest, examination and ridicule certainly seemed not to be a warlike king. Some may well have shifted allegiance under the influence of this disappointment.

It may be, too, that many of those who greeted him with acclamation on what we call Palm Sunday were pilgrims from

Galilee and the remoter parts of Judea, where His fame was great. Some of them might have departed on Friday, leaving Jesus' fate in the hands of the more volatile, cynical crowds of the urban townspeople.

It must be supposed, also, that the mass of the people who had previously acclaimed Jesus would in many cases have been of the type reluctant to get involved in raucous demonstrations such as that which took place before Pilate's judgment seat. It would have been easy, in any event, in a great urban center such as Jerusalem, for the leaders of the movement against Jesus to have organized, and paid for, a claque to take the lead in the mob's demonstrations—and what mob is not rather easily susceptible to the inflammatory cries of a small but organized group of fanatical hangers-on?

These considerations lead me to suppose that the mob before Pilate was by no means necessarily expressing the preponderant view of the people of Jerusalem or of Jewry. Jesus' ministry and miracles had made too deep an imprint to have been so suddenly and completely deprived of all influence on people's minds.

More central and much less easily resolved is the question, what went through Jesus' mind as He was questioned, mocked, whipped, struck, and shuttled back and forth from one jurisdiction to another? He did not deny most of the charges, even in the "loaded" form in which they were put. Some He even confirmed. Often He was silent, inscrutably so. One would say from the accounts that He bore Himself with stoicism, resignation, and royal dignity in the face of humiliation, extreme danger, and personal abuse. We have to remember that as Immanuel He had already accepted God's will in this matter. He knew what was coming and why it was coming, that He was steadily moving toward an act of supreme sacrifice "for many" and "for the remission of sins."

We must look ahead to Jesus' prayer on the Cross for the

forgiveness of His tormenters and judges and all their agents. It cannot be doubted that He was filled with pity and compassion for these human enemies whose free will had led them to choose so evil a course. The One who was to be the sacrificial lamb was no doubt in the most intense and fervent inner prayer to Immanuel's Father, seeking for the strength to undergo what was to come. Thus it is that one gets the feeling of a man distant, aloof, answering minimally and somewhat fitfully the questions put to Him, already more than a little apart from this world.

Altogether, the events from Judas's kiss to Pilate's judgment constitute a somber picture of heroic tragedy for Immanuel, but tragedy borne with the overwhelming dignity to be expected from God in the shambles of human error.

20
"Death"

The earthly end approached. On Golgotha, they nailed Jesus to a Cross, driving huge spikes through His wrists and through His feet. The agony defies rational thought. Then the Cross was raised and implanted in the ground, to be looked upon with jeering laughter by His enemies, with scornful indifference by the soldiers who were simply doing their duty for far-off Caesar, and with searing emotion by His mother, His dear disciple John, and the other faithful few who had summoned the courage to be present.

There were a few last attempts to humiliate this man whose ministry had been so gentle, so healing, so compassionate, but so threatening to the Establishment of Israel. A mocking sign was put over His head to ridicule His claim to "kingship." Under His pain-racked eyes, the soldiers rolled the dice to see who would get His garments. Onlookers taunted Him, jeering that He should save Himself, this wonder-worker who was so powerful and had saved so many others from disease and death. When He cried out in an agony of thirst, He was offered vinegar to drink.

Even in this dark hour of extreme pain and approaching death, there were three last evidences of His divine compassion and love. He called aloud on the Father to forgive all those who had done this thing, because they had done it in human ignorance of God's law of love. Next He called out to

John to take care of His weeping mother and told His mother to regard John henceforth as her son. And finally, touched by the last-minute faith in Him displayed by one of the two criminals crucified on either side of Him, He promised the man that he would go to paradise with Him that very day. Beset with incredible suffering, He yet thought of others, even His enemies.

The Cross on which He hung has long ago become the Christian symbol. We see it on and in our churches. We see it in cemeteries. We see it in art. We see it in jewelry, sometimes worn reverently but most often worn thoughtlessly and meaninglessly by all and sundry, even assaulting our eyes on the ears and around the necks of the stars of rock and roll with their flaunting immodesty of dress and gesture and their often indecent words. Yes, the Cross is very well known to us.

Often, too, we see the Cross portrayed a little more graphically as a Crucifix, with a figure affixed to it. Frequently the figure is stylized, without realism, without suffering. Sometimes, to be sure, it bears a twisted and pitiable figure, but the imagery is sparse and the repetition dulling.

In short, we talk about the Cross so much and see it so often that it has almost lost its power to move us. It has certainly lost its power, short of the most concentrated effort of will, to convey the full truth of the sacrifice and suffering it represents. It is even probable that many of us, tenderhearted in the face of suffering, prefer to blot out the pain of that moment and dwell only on the abstract benefit it brought to mankind.

On rare occasions we are forced to face the starkness of that fearful Crucifixion. Such a moment came to me once in the Swiss city of Lugano. I was visiting the Villa Favorita, where the remarkable Thyssen collection of art is displayed. Suddenly I came face to face with the suffering Christ. It was a painting by Donato Bramante, best known as the architect of St. Peter's in Rome. The painting is known under several titles, of which the most accurate is *Christ as the Man of Pain*. Curiously, it does not depict Jesus actually on the Cross, but rather as resurrected. Theologically, it cannot be fitted into either the Crucifixion or the Resurrection. Nevertheless, it depicts with wrenching vividness the terror and horror of the Crucifixion. The wound in the side is evident; the eyes are red-rimmed and bloodshot; the face is pallid and lined and haggard beyond description. Yet it is no travesty. It is reality as seen by a painter who must have immersed himself mercilessly in the imagination of what Christ suffered. I was transfixed for half an hour, realizing as never before what Jesus had done for me and for all mankind by accepting the Cross. I can never look with detachment or equanimity upon a Cross again.

Jesus hung there from nine in the morning until three in the afternoon. Many people doubtless came and went, for He was a well-known personage and a crucifixion was an event of interest, like a hanging in later ages or execution by guillotine during the French Revolution. There may well have been a Jewish Madame Defarge, sitting there placidly knitting and enjoying all the excitement! Yet He hung there for six hours, suffering the initial pain of the nails, then the pain of thirst, then the growing pain inflicted by gravity as it pulled and distorted His body. Perhaps a merciful sort of coma enveloped Him toward the end, from which He roused Himself just long enough to gasp, "It is finished." Jesus died.

A bright star and the song of angels had heralded His birth. Darkness accompanied His death. We are told that from noon on there was darkness over the land. One can make of this what one wants. Perhaps it was the darkness of grief and sorrow and pain. Perhaps it was an eclipse of the sun—but a solar eclipse lasts less than eight minutes. Perhaps it was the dark suffering of God for Immanuel. There were other strange concurrent portents. The earth quaked, rocks split open, graves were opened, and many bodies arose. The veil in the

Temple was split from top to bottom, the veil which screened from sight the Holy of Holies where the Ark of the Covenant had reposed until its destruction more than five centuries earlier.

Surely there are indications enough that something cosmic happened that Friday.

The soldiers forebore to break the legs as was customary, because "they saw that he was dead already" (Saint John 19:33). The body was reverently lowered and taken away for burial by Joseph of Arimathea, a devout disciple, who secretly went to Pilate for permission to do so. There also went Nicodemus, that same Nicodemus who was a Pharisee but who had sought one night to learn more of His message from Jesus, who had acknowledged that this Rabbi had come from God and that God was with Him, and who had been sufficiently impressed to stand up before his fellow Pharisees and contend that Jesus should not be judged and condemned until He had had a fair hearing. Just possibly Nicodemus can be considered to have been a Pharisee convert.

At any rate, Nicodemus now brought a quantity of spices to put in the winding sheet with the body, which was then laid in an unused but newly-hewn tomb in a nearby "garden." Unnamed women followed and observed these events. (Saints Matthew and Mark do name Mary Magdalene and another Mary as among these witnesses.) A little later the authorities posted a guard over the tomb.

A strange silence envelops the story at this point. Where did the disciples and other followers go, or where were they hiding? We are not told, but in all likelihood they were numb and crushed with despair. Their Master, their Rabbi, their comrade and Leader, even He whom they had finally acknowledged to be the Son of God, was dead. It seemed the end of all their hopes and dreams. Their small and human comprehension of this man had been stretched beyond the breaking point.

All the talk of rising again, all the talk of returning to the Father, all the talk of dying for the remission of sins—all this had gone over their heads. All they could now see was that Jesus had been nailed to a Cross and had died.

Immanuel? They had forgotten not only the teachings but also the prophecy. But God had not forgotten.

21
"He Is Risen"—Immanuel's Triumph

Now occurred perhaps the greatest and certainly the most productive cataclysm in history. Jesus' body, His temple, had been cruelly destroyed. But He had said that if this temple were destroyed He would raise it up again in three days. No one understood. There is no evidence that anyone even remembered—until later.

The body was entombed late on Friday. Friday night, Saturday, and Saturday night are blank pages in the record. But early on Sunday, apparently just as dawn was breaking, Mary Magdalene and other women approached the tomb to prepare the body more permanently. To their astonishment and consternation, the stone had been rolled back and the body was gone. The guards seem to have fled, but a young man (two, by some accounts) in dazzling white robes told them that their Lord was risen. This cryptic message sent them pell-mell back to Peter and the others in a wild mixture of fear, joy, and panic.

Peter and John ran at full speed to see for themselves and found that the news was true. One can imagine the excitement, the confusion, the doubts. Even the report from Mary Magdalene that she had actually met the Lord and He had spoken to her in the garden seems scarcely to have been taken in or was disbelieved at first or was lost in the general jumble of stupefying reports and speculation. One gets the impression of a disturbed anthill, with its occupants emerging in a frenzy and running seemingly wildly in every direction.

What happened in the intervening thirty-six hours? The answer to this greatest of all mysteries is forever hidden from us, or at least until that great day in heaven when perhaps all shall be revealed. On Friday Jesus is killed and entombed. On Sunday the tomb is empty and the Lord begins to appear and talk with His followers, albeit with an altered appearance. Something happened in between that is reported to have knocked the guards unconscious; they came to and fled and reported to the authorities and were told to spread the story that the disciples had stolen the body. Some people through the centuries have believed this propagandistic rumor and have considered the whole story of the Resurrection to be a fabrication out of whole cloth.

A half-century ago, one Frank Morison, an English lawyer and writer, a believer in Jesus but at first a nonbeliever in the transcendental Immanuel, set out to write a book proving the historicity of the last days of Jesus' life. He ended up by writing a book, *Who Moved the Stone?*, in which he proved in a rather convincing rational manner that Jesus did rise from the dead. It is a valuable contribution to thought about the subject, and rational human proof is not to be scorned by religion. Yet when all is said and done, belief in the Resurrection has to stem from faith, from that faith implanted in us by God's grace and really based on nothing more substantial than the some-times disjointed testimony of those who saw and talked with the risen Jesus or who knew such people. It may be, of course, that science and history will one day provide indisputable factual evidence.

Exactly what happened, therefore, we do not "know" with anything approaching certainty. Whatever it was, we also are in deepest ignorance of the *when* of it; at what point in the thirty-six-hour interlude did Immanuel rise to life again? Traditionally we have thought of it as having taken place early on the Sunday morning, perhaps just shortly before Mary Magdalene arrived. There is no absolute certainty about this. The Church teaches through its Apostles' Creed that at some point in this period "He descended into Hell." It is believed that Christ carried the Gospel of repentance and redemption to all the dead in "the place of departed spirits." This would most likely have been done in spirit, but it is certainly not inconceivable that it was done in the spiritualized Resurrection body. However, it must be noted that the men set to guard the tomb seem not to have reported what happened until Sunday morning, so it is rather unlikely that the earth quaked, the stone was removed, and Jesus walked out before the early morning hours of Sunday.

At any rate, I am impressed with the fact that too many people saw the post-Resurrection Jesus for the story to be pure fabrication. Mary Magdalene and the other women saw Him. Two disciples walking on the road to Emmaus saw Him. Ten of the disciples saw Him in Jerusalem when He suddenly appeared in their closed meeting room. Thomas saw Him and felt the wounds,[1] in the presence of the others. Seven of the disciples saw Him at the Sea of Tiberias and shared broiled fish with Him on the shore. Peter saw him. The Eleven together again saw Him in Galilee. He appeared to more than five hundred "of the brethren," according to Saint Paul, writing to the Church at Corinth only twenty years or so after the event. Saint Paul added that most of the five hundred were still alive when he wrote, and such a statement, if untrue, would have risked public controversy and denials; there is no historical record of such denials. The Lord was also seen by James.

These recorded appearances are too numerous to be swept under the rug of disbelief. Whoever would deny the

Resurrection must dispute incontrovertibly this impressive written record and testimony.

In short, Jesus Christ burst the bonds of corporeal death in some mighty and awesome act of divine will—and quite likely in full accordance with physical principles of which we are as yet unaware, or at best only dimly and imperfectly aware. The physical body was changed, but not beyond all possibility of recognition. The spirit was intact and still teaching and commissioning. This spirit/body behaved in unusual ways, apparently appearing where it would, at will, not stopped by doors or walls or distances. But it was there, acknowledged by many. Death could never again be final.

Through the centuries, the Christian Church has focussed on the Cross as the end, the triumph, the redemptive act. This emphasis is, in my opinion, somewhat distorted and incomplete. Without doubt, the death on the Cross *was* a redemptive sacrifice, a supreme act of divine self-abnegation, a uniquely sacrificial act by which God assumed all the sins of mankind—what a mountainous burden, putting Atlas's feat of strength to insignificance! But if this sacrifice unto death had been the end, how could it be said to have achieved anything? The sacrifice would have gone with Jesus into the grave, and there it would have stayed, useless to God or man. Having absorbed into Himself mankind and mankind's sins by His death, Christ then had to overcome what has never before or since been overcome: physical death. This was clearly necessary not only in order to provide the final testimony of His dual nature, but also in order to take back with Him to the Father in good time the human race, sinful but forgiven, to reunite God and man, separated since Eden.

Jesus dominated the dual nature in death. Immanuel dominated it in the triumph over death.

Note

1. Saint John's account (20:26–29) does not actually say that Thomas touched the Lord's wounds, but I have always liked to picture him as obeying the Lord's command to do so.

22

Return to the Father

A human cycle was ending. A baby had been born, prophesied to be and proclaimed to be "God with us." He had gone through a rather short but rich and even spectacular human life. He had ministered and taught and chastised. He had healed and fed and raised to life. He had died in agony and risen in splendid convulsion. For a brief period He had again met with and taught His disciples, especially the Chosen Eleven. His last words to them had included the command, thrice repeated, to "feed my sheep." He had given them their marching orders to preach to all the world His message of repentance and salvation. Now He had a sense of mission accomplished.

He led them out into the countryside (Saint Luke says near Bethany; Saint Matthew suggests it was in Galilee), and there He left them and disappeared from their sight in some mysterious way. To the eyes of the eleven disciples He rose into the air until He was veiled by a cloud—that same cloud that so often veils the glory, the brilliant splendor, of God, throughout the Scriptures. The description of this event is to be taken symbolically rather than literally. To the disciples it *seemed* as though He ascended "into the heavens," because they could find no other terms consonant with human experience and their theological understanding to describe what happened, what they saw.

The how and where and when of it are quite immaterial. Jesus Christ was gone. He returned to the Father who had sent Him and of whom He was, is, and always will be a part. Many questions do naturally arise. Had He been in heaven in the Godhead ever since His Resurrection, simply returning at will a few times to meet and converse with the disciples? Or was He, during the forty-day post-Resurrection period, in some kind of intermediate state, no longer of this world and its corruptible nature but not yet in the heaven of the incorruptible spirit? Did His nature, that duality of man and God, change at the Resurrection or at the Ascension? Did the man Jesus disappear for good when death was defeated, and was it Immanuel alone who appeared and spoke and ate during the forty days? How *shall* one describe the Being who was received into Heaven before the very eyes of eleven frightened, awestruck men? These are tantalizing questions, but useless. They defy analysis. They require no analysis. For thirty-three years He moved among men in a normal way. For forty days after His death He appeared and communicated in an intelligible way. At last, He left the earth for good as far as tangible presence is concerned, until the Second Coming which He promised.

We have remarked before upon the role that angels so often played in this singular history—at the Annunciation, at the birth, at the temptation, at the empty tomb. Now they appeared once more, as the disciples gaped unbelievingly upward. Don't be afraid, was the sense of their message. He has gone to Heaven, and one day He shall come again from there. Having heard this message, the disciples returned to Jerusalem, stunned, sorrowing, uncertain—but also hopeful.

Immanuel in human form had left this earth and mankind. It seemed the end. But there were still to be postscripts.

Note

A great deal has been written and said about the forty-day period after the Resurrection. The Church tends to teach us, and we tend commonly to understand, that the Ascension of our Lord took place forty days after His Resurrection and that the various appearances recorded in Scripture are, therefore, post-Resurrection and pre-Ascension. But the scriptural accounts of the Ascension vary dramatically. Mark and Luke place it on Easter Day itself, and Luke says it took place in Bethany, not Galilee.

It thus appears likely that there were more than one departures into "heaven" by way of an "Ascension" and that all the recorded appearances were of the glorified Christ, who had already been received back into God in glory. The details and variations in the scriptural accounts are numerous and fascinating. And there are also the many and believable postscriptural accounts of the Lord's appearances to man (e.g., Saint Teresa of Avila).

But I am not writing a theological treatise. I am telling the story of a life which includes death, Resurrection, Ascension, and personal appearances of the Risen Lord. He is with us in spirit and can be with us in his glorified person at any time until His final coming in great glory. That is all that counts.

23

Postscripts from Heaven

Back in Jerusalem after the Ascension, the Apostles remained closeted in an "upper room." There they lived in constant prayer, remembering the words and acts of the Lord, doubtless half-remembering and beginning to understand some of the forgotten or more perplexing incidents and teachings. Perhaps for the first time Peter, James, and John depicted to the others the incredible scene at the Lord's Transfiguration. Perhaps they all reviewed together the various miracles and the words given to them after the Resurrection. In any event, they had lost their bearings and were undoubtedly praying fervently for some guidance.

Guidance came in almost one week's time. It was the day of Pentecost, a Jewish Feast celebrated fifty days after Passover. Matthias had meanwhile been chosen by a combination of election and lot to fill Judas Iscariot's place, so they were again Twelve. They were "all" together, possibly still in the upper room, possibly in some of the Temple precincts, and the evidence suggests that they were a fairly numerous crowd. They were in a state of some excitement and expectation, awaiting something but not at all sure what. They remembered the pledge of Jesus that He would send the "promise of the Father" to them so that they would be "endued with power from on high" (Saint Luke 24:49).

Suddenly two strange happenings took place. The calmness of the morning air was broken by the sound of a great wind rushing by, and in almost the same moment they saw little tongues or plumes of fire come to rest on the heads of all. We are dealing here with a situation much like that at the Ascension—men keyed up almost to the point of trance or hysteria, suffering an experience without precedent, an experience which they had no means to describe realistically. There can be no doubt that something happened, something quite extraordinary and unprecedented, something they understood as coming from outside this mundane earth. The event clearly partook of the transcendental—a word not much used in our age but a word signifying a reality which has never ceased to exist.

This unique event on Pentecost, while bearing the marks of the supernatural, was understood by all those present, and was forevermore to be understood, as a kind of baptism of power and strength and understanding given by God, with whom they now knew their late Master to be indissolubly one.

Jesus was gone. Immanuel was with them. They were transformed. This was postscript number one, and perhaps the more important postscript in a general spiritual sense. It bore the seal and signature of the Holy Ghost.

I like to think of another happening as a second postscript, this one more personal and coming directly from Immanuel Himself, some few days or weeks later.

There was a young fanatic named Saul, who threw himself with unreserved zeal into the fight to eradicate these Christians, subverters of the traditional faith of Israel. He was present as an enthusiastic partisan at the murderous stoning of Stephen, one of the first seven ordained deacons; those who did the stoning gave their outer robes into Saul's keeping so that they could give themselves more freely to their bloody task. Saul became a sort of vigilante, a vengeful tracker-down of Christians, whom he ruthlessly seized and imprisoned. Finally he sought papers from the high priest which would give him the power to go to Damascus to hunt down the members of the Christian community there.

Saul got the authority he sought. He set off toward Damascus, full of rage and threats. There was unexpected intervention from on high. As Saul neared the gate in the walls of Damascus, an unbearably dazzling light struck him blind and he fell cowering to earth. A voice, heard also by his companions, thundered the question: "why persecutest thou me?" (Acts 9:4.) Though dazed, Saul was yet curious enough to ask who spoke to him. The answer was: "Jesus, whom thou persecutest" (Acts 9:5). Some cryptic directions were given for him to follow. The blinded man obeyed to the letter.

Interesting questions tantalize our minds about this event. Is it to be classed as a miracle or as simply one more post-Resurrection appearance; of course, all the post-Resurrection appearances were miracles as far as our human understanding goes. If a miracle, some might ask, was it not an example of a miracle used as punishment, contrary to my earlier assertion that Jesus never used miracles as punishment? If ever anyone deserved punishment, it was Saul, for his brutal and persistent persecution of the Christians. But I look upon the temporary blinding at the Damascus gate not as punishment but as a corrective reproach, a call to arms, a means of transformation, a rebirth. God had a use for Saul as a man of full vigor, not as a blinded man. Therefore he adopted a striking measure of reproach and conversion, not a crippling punishment.

This, then, was the second postscript and the last direct message from Immanuel recorded in the Bible. The Son's intervention in this case gave us Saint Paul, one of the greatest of all Christian Apostles—tireless, wide-ranging, fearless, a prolific interpreter of the Christian message.

As the vision and the voice at the Damascus gate disappear, we lose sight for the last time in the Scriptures of Immanuel as a person perceived to be present in some physical sense. The prophets and angels had said he was coming to be with us as God. The entire record of His life corroborates the fact that He *was* with us as God and man, divinity and humanity conjoined. His death, Resurrection, and Ascension stamp Him clearly and finally as Immanuel. Then, as if reluctant to leave us and desirous of giving us two last signs, He reached out from heaven twice more, with transcendental power and authority.

Whose biography could this be other than Immanuel's, the story of God's life while he walked the earth for a brief space, sharing our human experience? Whose Truth could this be other than God's?